The
Louisiana Purchase

THE LOUISIANA PURCHASE

973.4

by Robert Tallant

ILLUSTRATED BY
Warren Chappell

Landmark
BOOKS

RANDOM HOUSE · NEW YORK

4 264

Contents

The
Louisiana Purchase

THOMAS JEFFERSON
of *Virginia*

1: Meet Thomas Jefferson

W HEN THOMAS JEFFERSON BECAME PRESI-
dent of the United States on March 4, 1801, more
than twenty-five years had passed since he had
written the Declaration of Independence. Perhaps 1776 did not seem so long ago to him for
the years between had been busy, stirring ones.

During that time the American Revolution had been fought and won.* Jefferson had enjoyed a long career. Once he had tried to retire to Monticello, his beautiful home in Virginia. He had hoped then to be free of politics and public office. But now he had been elected the third President of his country.

He would fulfill his duties here in the new capital of Washington where he was about to begin the speech accepting the highest office in the country. At that moment, many wearisome thoughts must have been in his mind. Standing on the platform built for the inauguration ceremonies, he must have known it would not be an easy role he was about to play. He must have thought of the wars in Europe and of all the land on this continent that still belonged to foreign powers. He must have known that both of these situations presented problems that he must now face. He must have realized how quickly this young nation might lose the freedom she had fought hard to win.

Besides these dangers there were others within the country itself. The party that had elected

*You can read more about this period in another Landmark Book, *Our Independence and the Constitution* by Dorothy Canfield Fisher.

Jefferson was called the Republican Party, although it was not the same Republican Party we have today. The other party was called the Federalist Party. The Federalists hated Jefferson and most of the principles in which he believed.

There were smaller groups against him, too. There were even people in the nation who wanted the United States to have a king and a system of royalty. They thought the American republic could not last and that democracy was a foolish dream that would not work.

Yet Jefferson's speech was strong and hopeful. "Let us unite with one mind and one heart," he urged his listeners. And at the end he said:

"I know, indeed, that some honest men fear that a republican government cannot be strong; that this government is not strong enough. But would the honest patriot, in the full tide of successful experiment, abandon this government which has so far kept us free and firm . . . ?"

He said much else, most of it meaning that Americans must work together to give democracy a chance.

Thomas Jefferson was a great man. Some people think he was the greatest man of his period, perhaps the greatest in all American history. He was certainly a man of extraordinary intelligence. He seems to have been able to do nearly everything and to do it all well. He was not only a statesman. He was also a farmer, an architect, an engineer, a lawyer, a scholar, a philosopher, and a fine writer and orator.

He had been born in 1743, so when he became President he was almost fifty-eight years old. Nearly all his life had been devoted to his country.

It has been said that Jefferson would have preferred another kind of life. He wanted to devote himself to his great farm in his native state of Virginia, which he loved above everything but his country. He had, as an architect, designed his large and handsome home, still one of the most beautiful houses in America. Because it was built high on a hill, Jefferson called his home "Monticello," which means "little mountain."

As an inventor and an engineer he designed numerous improvements for his house and farm. In his home he had a fine library where he spent as much time as possible, reading his books and writing letters.

But most of all he loved his farm, every inch

of the soil and everything that grew out of it. It has been said that he watched for the appearance of each new leaf on a plant, for every blossom as it appeared in the spring. He was interested in the birds as they came to Monticello at the end of winter and left again in the late fall. He often wrote about these things in his letters to members of his family and to his friends.

In appearance, Jefferson was tall, thin, and lank. As a youth his freckled and sunburned face had been topped with a thatch of red hair. Now, as he took office as President, he was dressed in what was considered an old-fashioned style.

Perhaps his clothing told something about Jefferson, for he was a thoughtful, quiet man. He hated wars and loved peace, but he believed firmly in fighting for freedom when it was necessary. During his life he saw a great deal of war and very little of peace, both in this country and in other lands.

It was impossible for this quiet man to live the life of a Virginia gentleman farmer. He was too important; that period in American history was too important. When the tyranny of British rule drove the American colonies to revolt, Jefferson was one of the leaders in all that had to be done. He worked along with George Washington, John Adams, Benjamin Franklin,* and the other great men who took part in creating a nation.

With amendments by Franklin and Adams, he put into the beautiful words of the Declaration of Independence the feeling of most American leaders toward British rule. He expressed the American need for founding a free country, a new kind of country.

After President George Washington took office, Jefferson went to France as Minister from the United States. There he saw, as he had seen it in his own country, a need for freedom. When the French Revolution began on July 14, 1789, Jefferson's sympathies were with the people and against their rulers. The French people felt this so strongly and his beliefs and principles were so admired by them that he has been called "the godfather of the French Revolution." But, although he was with the French people, he hated the bloodshed that took place and the terror that lasted so long.

In 1789, when Jefferson returned to this coun-

*You can read more about this famous American in another Landmark Book, *Ben Franklin of Old Philadelphia* by Margaret Cousins.

try, President Washington made him Secretary of State. After Washington retired Jefferson tried to retire, too. But it was not for long. John Adams was elected President, with Jefferson his Vice-President. In the next election Thomas Jefferson was chosen President of his country—the country he had helped make a nation.

We must remember that it was "his country" in a very special sense. It had been founded on the principles of his own Declaration of Independence. Its highest laws were those of the Constitution he had helped compose and which was to him a sacred document. So in a way this United States was partly his own creation.

Now, elected President by the people, he would do everything in his power to make it stronger, better, richer, more secure. There were many threats against it, many dangers to overcome.

Yet, at the time of his election, Jefferson probably had no thought of increasing the nation's size. In fact most people thought the United States was already huge in land area, almost too big to be governed easily. Much of it was still a vast wilderness. Distances were great, and travel difficult.

There was only one place on the whole North

American continent and outside the boundaries of the country that did worry Jefferson. That was New Orleans, the small but important port down at the mouth of the Mississippi River. New Orleans was the capital of the immense Colony of Louisiana, which stretched from the Gulf of Mexico to the Canadian border on the other side of the Mississippi from the United States.

All Louisiana, including the port of New Orleans, was in the possession of Spain when Jefferson became President in 1801. Jefferson did not fear Spain. Yet he knew that whatever nation owned New Orleans could control the Mississippi River and all the commerce on the river. Such a nation, if it chose, could invade the United States in time of war, or at least close the port of New Orleans to American exports and damage the nation greatly. Jefferson knew, too, that Napoleon Bonaparte, the new tyrant rising to power in Europe, must be watching New Orleans, which had belonged to France not so long before.

Yet for the moment Jefferson had another problem that seemed more important than Louisiana and its owners. This was the problem of the raids and crimes being committed against American ships by the Barbary pirates.

These Barbary pirates operated out of three ports on the coast of North Africa—Algiers, Tripoli, and Tunis. They were fierce and murderous criminals who attacked ships, robbed them of merchandise, and often carried off crews and passengers to be sold into slavery. The pirates were paid tribute—a kind of blackmail—by many European nations, so that their ships might pass in freedom through the Mediterranean Sea.

Now these pirates were threatening the ships of the young United States. They asked for such large sums in exchange for the safety of our ships, that we could not afford to meet their demands. Both President Washington and President Adams had signed treaties with them and sent them money, but the treaties were never kept and the money sent was never enough. American ships had been seized; many American citizens had vanished forever into a life of slavery and torture.

For instance, in October 1800, the Dey of Algiers had forced a United States man-of-war, which was named the *George Washington,* to take down the proud American flag and raise that of Algiers. Then the captain and crew were made to sail their ship to Constantinople under escort, where the Americans were presented to the Sultan as slaves.

When this news reached the United States the government officials were outraged. President John Adams made violent protests, but they were useless. More money was sent to Algiers, but this was not the American way of dealing with barbarians.

Then, almost as Jefferson took office as President, the Pasha of Tripoli declared war on the United States because he had not received as much blackmail money as he demanded. American ships were attacked ruthlessly.

To deal with the matter Jefferson summoned his cabinet and spoke before Congress about a possible course of action. At once he received permission to send warships into the Mediterranean. There was fighting with the pirates, but little good was accomplished. It was to be 1805 before Jefferson secured a sound treaty from Tripoli and 1816 before all the trouble was ended. But of course that is another story. It is mentioned here only because it was one of the new President's most troublesome problems when he took office.

Meanwhile, Jefferson was giving thought to New Orleans. His ear was also turned toward the rumors and gossip coming from Europe.

This period in the world's history was a time of many changes. The new President realized it was his job to guide the United States safely through whatever changes were to come. No doubt Thomas Jefferson, with his brilliant mind and piercing vision, knew the nation would expand somewhat one day, but probably he thought there would be little increase in its territory during his own life. He did hope that New Orleans might become an American port, for that city was vital to the country's needs.

Certainly he could not guess what was on the very next pages of history. Certainly he did not know that he was about to play a role in America's story that would be in its way as important as the role he had played in the Revolution. What was about to happen would have seemed fantastic, even to Jefferson.

2: *Jefferson and His United States*

IN 1801, WHEN THOMAS JEFFERSON TOOK HIS oath of office as President of the United States, in what was then called Washington City, the nation was less than a third of its present size. It stretched from the Atlantic Ocean to the Mississippi River and from the Canadian border to the Floridas.

There were two Floridas then, called West Florida and East Florida. East Florida became, in a general way, the State of Florida we know today. West Florida, for the most part, became in time the southern portions of Alabama and Mississippi, and a little of Louisiana.

This United States was already large, but we must remember big portions of it were still uninhabited and other parts were very thinly populated. Most people lived in the northeast and along the Atlantic coast where all the cities and most of the big towns were located.

Much of the rest of the country was wilderness, with scattered settlers who had come to live in the forests, hills, and mountains. These pioneers had built homes and farms and had established trading posts. It is curious now to remember that what became the State of Tennessee, for instance, was once called the "Southwest Territory."

By 1801—the year of Jefferson's inauguration—the thirteen original United States had increased to sixteen. Three new states had been carved out and given names and boundaries. These were Vermont, which became a state in 1791, Kentucky, in 1792, and Tennessee, 1796.

Still, the most important part of Thomas Jefferson's United States stretched from New England down through the Carolinas and about as far west as the present western border of Virginia.

At that time there were no cities and few towns of large population that were not close to the Atlantic seaboard. New York was a thriving seaport, as was Boston. Until the year before Jefferson's election as President Philadelphia had been the nation's capital. Virginia had no cities, but it contained great and prosperous plantations, as did the Carolinas.

Even Washington, when it became the capital in June 1800, was an almost empty tract of land on the Potomac, partially a swamp, and considered by most persons an unfit place to live. When Jefferson went there to serve as the nation's leader the only buildings were the half-finished White House, the unfinished Capitol, and a dozen or so other buildings. Most of the latter were boarding houses where Senators, Congressmen, and government employees lived while in Washington. In order to get about the capital while he was President Jefferson usually rode about on horseback!

In 1801 the United States contained slightly more than five million persons, of whom perhaps a million were Negro slaves. Philadelphia was the largest city in the country, with a population of about seventy thousand. New York had about sixty thousand, and Boston about twenty-five thousand. The largest town in what was then called the "west" was Cincinnati, Ohio, where lived some fifteen thousand persons.

Large areas of United States territory were still inhabited by unfriendly Indian tribes who fought the white men whenever possible.* The powerful and fierce Creeks and Cherokees, the Choctaws and Chickasaws, lived in what were to become the States of Alabama, Mississippi, and parts of Tennessee and Kentucky. There were Shawnees, Miamis, Wyandots, and other tribes in what would become Michigan, Indiana, Illinois, and Wisconsin.

Every westward and southward movement meant dangerous encounters with these tribes, who would surrender their land only when driven back by overpowering odds. In some cases they outnumbered the white settlers inching into their country. At times they would retreat only

*You can read more about this period in another Landmark Book, *Daniel Boone* by John Mason Brown.

to return again and again. Life in these wildernesses meant being on constant guard against
Indian attack.

Another reason for the delay in settling the
country was, of course, the difficulties of dis-
tance and travel. It is said, for instance, that no
one could travel faster than four miles an hour
between Maine and Maryland by stagecoach.
There were no railroads then, no good roads of
any sort, almost no bridges upon which to cross
rivers and streams.

Wagons, coaches, and carriages were always
breaking down, getting stuck in mud and mire,
and suffering other accidents. Travelers must
stop overnight at inns or at the homes of friends.
Carrying food for both humans and horses presented problems.

These traveling conditions had an influence
on the customs and habits of the people of the
United States. People living in one part of the
country knew little about their countrymen in
the other sections.

We hear much of pioneers and the early settlers
who roamed this great country, but actually they
were the exceptions. Most people stayed at home,
interested only in what went on in their own

communities. Each state was almost a little country unto itself. If a stranger asked a man what he was he usually replied that he was a Virginian or a Pennsylvanian.

Newspapers were few and most of the news they printed was about local affairs. All news traveled slowly, so that little interest was aroused in happenings outside a person's native state. Most news was brought by the comparatively few men who did travel, and when it came it was something of an event. Yet a man living in North Carolina, for instance, gave little thought to what was taking place in Massachusetts. That was a far, far journey away, and he was never likely to go there.

In Jefferson's day his own Virginia was the most thickly populated of all the states, for it contained nearly a million white inhabitants. Also, it had given the nation many of its greatest statesmen, for George Washington, James Monroe, John Randolph, and James Madison were all Virginians.

Virginia was an old and civilized community when Jefferson was born. Early settlers had chosen it as a place to live because of the fertility of its soil, its mild climate, and its beauty. Those who had chosen Virginia as a home had chosen wisely, for its people were prosperous compared to those of most other states. The wealthier men were very rich indeed for their day, although most of this wealth was in land, in tobacco and other crops, and in slaves, as was usual at the time.

Life was good in Virginia. People had fine, beautiful houses on their huge plantations. For most of them life was full and rich. There were many balls in the great houses. Horse racing and hunting were popular sports. There was a high level of education, and much importance was placed on fine manners among the wealthy plantation owners. Travelers from Europe, in their letters about life in Virginia, told how closely it resembled that of English country gentlemen. But Virginia was always democratic and it did not have the great differences in class that were features of life in England and the other countries of Europe.

For a man did not have to be born on one of the great tobacco plantations to reach the top in Virginia. It was not only a state of fine plantations, but one in which the law and politics were thought to be of major importance. Any young

man who showed talent was given his chance to
rise. Henry Clay, who became one of our greatest statesmen, was first a mill boy and then a
clerk in his early days in Virginia. Patrick Henry
had been poor in his youth. Even the father of
Thomas Jefferson was an uneducated man, although he had prospered and owned some land
when Jefferson was born.

So this was the United States that Jefferson
knew when he became President of the United
States. It was a place of many differences, a huge
country for its time, with vast distances, wide,
uninhabited spaces, and great wildernesses. We
cannot be surprised that no one thought it would
spread much more, at least not soon. There was
still too much to be done with what had already
come under the leadership of the government
at Washington.

That gigantic country across the Mississippi
River called Louisiana, most of it still unexplored and unknown, was farther away from the
centers of civilization in the United States of
that time than is any country in the world today
from any other. This is true if we measure distances not in miles, but in time and in ease of
travel.

3: *The Land Across the Mississippi*

THE COLONY THEN CALLED LOUISIANA HAD belonged to Spain since 1763. Before that it had belonged to France.

French power in North America came to an end as a result of the Seven Years War. By what was called the Treaty of Paris, signed in 1763,

France had to surrender to Great Britain all her land east of the Mississippi River. But before this treaty was signed the French king, Louis XV, presented Louisiana, including what was called the "Isle of Orleans" to his cousin, Charles III, the king of Spain. In that way Louis XV cheated England out of Louisiana. He also repaid Spain for her losses in the Seven Years War, a war in which Spain had fought at the side of France.

But no Frenchmen had ever forgotten the loss of the Louisiana territory. Neither had the French citizens of New Orleans, the capital city on the "Isle of Orleans." In fact the citizens of New Orleans had rioted in 1768 when Spanish authorities came to take charge of the colony. Later they had become used to Spanish rule. But the French still remembered that Louisiana had been theirs. By 1792 they were dreaming of taking it back. When Napoleon Bonaparte became ruler of France he was fascinated with this idea. He began making some plans.

Because no one knew much about the land that was called Louisiana—not the Americans, nor the French, nor even the Spanish who owned it—there was an argument about its western boundary. All the nations agreed that Louisiana was bordered on the north by Canada, on the south by the Gulf of Mexico, on the east by the Mississippi River; but exactly where did the territory end in the west?

The generally accepted western boundary followed the Rocky Mountains to the north and then a rough line that ran along the Sabine River to the south. Yet there were those who went so far as to include Texas in Louisiana. Some maps, still in existence, show New Orleans as the capital of Texas!

If the United States was slow in becoming interested in Louisiana as a whole, there was one part of it, besides New Orleans, in which many Americans were very much interested. That was the Mississippi River. It was of special interest to the settlers of such states as Kentucky and Tennessee, whose only way to sell their produce was to ship it down the river by barge and flatboat. There it might be loaded on ships and reach the sea, or, in some cases, it might be sold in New Orleans itself.

When Great Britain and France had owned all the North American continent they had granted each other the right to free navigation of the river. After Louisiana became Spanish and the eastern part of the lower half of the continent became the United States, all this changed. The Spanish were jealous of the Americans and thought of them as dangerous rivals.

Through the years the Spaniards often closed the Mississippi to American shipping. At other times the Spanish officials in New Orleans would charge a tax for admitting American goods to their city. This tax, or duty, was so high that the Americans could not afford to pay it. Then their produce would rot on their barges at the New Orleans wharves because the Spanish would not let them unload. Once a group of Kentuckians threatened to take their rifles and shoot up New Orleans in revenge for this kind of treatment.

This came to an end in 1797. That year a treaty was signed with the Spanish which allowed the Americans to use the western half of the Mississippi River. The treaty had been drawn up in 1791 by Thomas Jefferson. Then he had been Secretary of State under President George Washington.

After this some Americans moved across the Mississippi into Spanish territory and settled on the river's western banks. American pioneers had tried this before, but the Spanish outposts along the river had usually driven them out. Sometimes the Spanish had even set the Indians against them. They would bribe the Indians to attack the pioneers and many Americans had been massacred. After 1797 the Spanish stopped this, but they still did not like American settlers on their land.

But this did not mean that many Americans were living in Louisiana when Jefferson became President in 1801. Indeed the great land was almost empty of white men of any nationality. There were a good many Indian tribes, scattered farms and settlements belonging to Americans and, to the north, other farms owned by French Canadians, who had drifted down from Canada.

There were few towns. St. Louis was a fur-trading post with a population of little more than 800. There were scattered here and there a few smaller settlements — Natchitoches, Arkansas Post, New Madrid, St. Charles, Carondelet, Cape Girardeau, and others.

The principal town, the only one that might be called a city, was of course New Orleans, which boasted a population of about 12,000.

More than one-third of the white population of Louisiana lived either in New Orleans or St. Louis, but New Orleans was much the larger of the two. It had been the capital of the colony under both French and Spanish regimes, and it was much more important than any city with an equally small population would be today.

It is necessary to know something about New Orleans and why it was so important if we are to understand how the whole colony of Louisiana became in time a part of the United States.

4: *New Orleans, Capital City*

JEFFERSON HAD BEEN THINKING ABOUT
New Orleans for a long time. He had considered
it a dangerous spot back in the days when he
had been Secretary of State in George Washington's cabinet. He had worked then to settle
American rights to use it as a port. The Missis-

sippi was of no use to anyone without New Orleans. In that fact lay Spain's power in North America. Any country owning that port would possess some power over the United States.

Later, in a letter to Robert R. Livingston, the American Minister to France, Jefferson wrote, "There is on this globe one single spot, the possessor of which is our natural and habitual enemy. It is New Orleans."

Unlike all the rest of Louisiana, New Orleans had long been a civilized community. It had already had a long history before France gave it to Spain. The city had been founded in 1718 by Jean Baptiste Le Moyne de Bienville, a French soldier and explorer. It had remained French until 1766. When the Spanish had come to claim it and to establish their rule and laws they had been compelled to take it by force, for its citizens were French in language, in thought, and in feeling. They remained so for a long time after Spain took over the rule of the city.

New Orleans had always been entirely different from any other part of the country. It was far from the Atlantic seaboard, a world removed from New England, even from Virginia. The people of the original colonies that broke away from Great Britain were, for the most part, of English, Scotch, Irish, German, and Dutch descent, with some Frenchmen among them. But New Orleans in its early days was all French.

Bienville had laid out the city as a military post; then it began to grow. The French soldiers sent home for French brides. Younger generations began to grow up.

Soon New Orleans had schools, a theater, ballrooms. There was the fine St. Louis Cathedral, where everyone went to church.

Some people of other nationalities came to New Orleans, but they intermarried with the French. In no time the newcomers, too, were French, or at least their children seemed to be. Everyone spoke French. If a New Orleans citizen traveled in those days it was usually to France, or perhaps to the French colonies in the West Indies.

New Orleans was a strange and varied city. It was dirty and for more than the first hundred years of its life it was probably the most unhealthful city on the North American continent. It suffered from plagues and epidemics of yellow fever and cholera. The streets were of mud and the sidewalks were only wooden planks on which people tried to walk as best they could. Open gutters were filled with filthy, stagnant water.

The people of early New Orleans faced other kinds of perils, too. They fought off Indians and uprisings of slaves. Many of the latter were savages from Africa, wild, untamed, and filled with fierce and natural hatred of the white men who had forced them into slavery.

From the first days of its history, New Orleans was a port. All kinds of people came up the river from the Gulf of Mexico, some of them French. These were always welcomed. But the crews of the ships were a tough lot. Some were really pirates.

Down the Mississippi came other boats, the flatboats bringing crude backwoodsmen, Kentuckians who were rough and always eager for a fight. To most Orleanians these were typical Americans—the only Americans they ever saw. For such people, the Orleanians had little love.

So whatever its actual population was at any time in those days, there were always many more people in the city than really lived there. It was not only a port, but a trading center and a market place as well. French, Spanish, Americans, Indians, and Negroes walked the streets and filled the public square, called the Place d'Armes, near the river. Taverns and coffee houses and all public places were always filled to the point of bursting. It was lively, noisy, dirty and exciting.

Although Louisiana became Spanish in 1763, when Louis XV gave the colony to Spain, nothing was changed for some time. But in 1764 word of the new Spanish ownership reached New Orleans. Shock swept through the town.

It seemed terrible to the inhabitants that France and Louis XV, the king upon whom the citizens of New Orleans looked as their ruler, had given the city and its people to Spain.

For a while nothing happened. No Spanish ships appeared in the Mississippi River; no Spanish authorities arrived to take charge of the capital city. It was as if neither Spain nor France cared about it or thought it of any importance. In a way this was true. Both countries were occupied with their constant wars. Treaties were signed, there would be a brief peace, then another war with another country.

Two years later, in 1766, Don Antonio de Ulloa, the Spanish commissioner, arrived at the New Orleans wharves with his aides. He presented letters and documents instructing the New

Orleans officials, who were still Frenchmen, to turn over the city. A pompous and demanding person, the new commissioner immediately earned the hatred of the people of New Orleans. But, for the moment, they gave way. Ulloa took charge and the Frenchmen let him have his place as head of the colony.

At once there were changes. These were many and so sudden that French New Orleans trembled with anger and resentment. All laws became Spanish laws, the money became Spanish money. There was even an attempt to force Orleanians to speak Spanish, but that never worked. Instead, the Spaniards had to learn to speak French so that they could be understood.

Beneath the surface the citizens of the city grumbled and gossiped. This grew until the Spaniards became extremely uncomfortable. They knew the hatred of the Orleanians had become widespread. They heard it in their ears like the humming of thousands of bees.

On October 28, 1768 the citizens of New Orleans held a mass meeting. They demanded the expulsion of Ulloa and the other Spaniards. That night a distinguished citizen, Joseph Roy Villeré, led four hundred men armed with rifles and swords in an attack upon the Tchoupitoulas Gate. This was a Spanish garrison on the Mississippi.

The Spaniards fled for their lives. Ulloa, his family, his officers and aides, boarded a Spanish ship tied up at the dock, hoping to be safe. The Orleanians, carrying torches and flares, cut the ship loose from its mooring. At dawn Ulloa found himself and his officials floating down the Mississippi toward the Gulf of Mexico. Ulloa did not go back. He went to Cuba.

With the Spaniards gone — forever, it was hoped — New Orleans citizens appointed Villeré their temporary leader and made plans to govern themselves and the rest of the colony. There was even talk of founding a Republic of Louisiana! But not everyone agreed on this. In their hearts many Orleanians wanted to return to French rule.

Also, we must remember that this was ten years before the American Revolution.* Many citizens of New Orleans feared that Great Britain, still ruler of the thirteen colonies, would send ships up the Mississippi and seize the city.

*You can read more about this period in another Landmark Book, *Paul Revere and the Minute Men* by Dorothy Canfield Fisher.

The debate continued for months. During this time New Orleans and Louisiana were completely free from foreign rule of any kind. Some men thought the Spanish would never come back. Others defied them to come back.

But at dawn on July 24, 1769 news reached the town that twenty-four Spanish men-of-war had passed the mouth of the river and were on their way to New Orleans.

The fleet lingered at the mouth of the river but did not reach New Orleans until early in August. On the day of its arrival every Orleanian who could do so left his house and business and stood waiting upon the levees along the Mississippi. Some men wanted to fight, to surrender the city to this second Spanish invasion only with their lives. But nothing happened.

There could be no opposition, for at that time the entire population, including women, children, and slaves numbered only a little more than 3000. The Spanish ships had brought 2600 seasoned soldiers. Resistance would have been suicidal.

The leader of the Spaniards was Count Alexander O'Reilly, Spain's most illustrious general. On August 18 he ordered the removal of the French flag which Orleanians had been flying in the Place d'Armes and replaced it with the flag of Spain. He replaced French laws with Spanish laws and tightened them severely, so that the citizens of the town would know who was ruler.

O'Reilly became one of the most hated men in the history of New Orleans. At his direction the leaders of the group which had revolted against Ulloa were placed under arrest and brought to trial. Six were executed and six put in prison.

Villeré died, but a mystery will always surround his death. O'Reilly said the rebel leader flew into such a fit of rage at the retaking of the city by the Spaniards that he dropped dead of a heart attack. The Orleanians said Villeré had been taken aboard one of the Spanish ships and murdered. There was even a story that Madame Villeré, his wife, learning her husband had been arrested and taken aboard a frigate, rowed out to the ship in a skiff. Coming alongside, she begged and pleaded for her husband's life. In answer the Spaniards tossed her a bloody shirt torn with the points of daggers.

Whether this and the other stories that were

told about the Spaniards were true or not, most Orleanians believed them. They grumbled and cursed the Spanish. They nicknamed the leader "Bloody" O'Reilly and even "Cannibal" O'Reilly. But there was nothing they could do.

Fortunately O'Reilly only stayed in New Orleans a year. His conquest complete, his work done, Spain recalled him for duties that were considered more important. He was replaced by a much milder and more tolerant governor, Don Luis de Unzaga. Unzaga did much good for the city. He relaxed many of the stern Spanish laws. He increased the shipping and the business going on at the port. More people came to live in New Orleans and the city prospered.

When the American Revolution broke out the citizens of New Orleans took very little interest in it, but the Spanish officials did. Eager to see England defeated, they allowed munitions and other supplies to pass through the city to be carried to the Atlantic colonies. American agents were allowed to establish bases in the port. By now the governor was Don Bernardo de Galvez, who was popular and well liked in New Orleans.

In ten years a lot can happen, and during that time New Orleans had decided Spanish rule was not so bad after all. Many of the Spanish soldiers who had come to the city married French New Orleans girls, and in a strange way New Orleans quickly absorbed the Spanish. The law and the money might be Spanish, but that was about all. The customs, the language, even the cooking remained French. The child of a Spaniard and a French mother seemed completely French. Some of the Spanish even changed their names so that they would sound French. And the French always far outnumbered the Spanish.

One reason for this was the French Revolution. After it began on July 14, 1789 many French aristocrats fled France. A number of them went to New Orleans where feeling for the aristocrats was strong. When Louis XVI and his queen, Marie Antoinette, lost their heads on the guillotine, New Orleans wept, for Louis had been considered by most people a mild and rather gentle king.

New Orleans had other troubles during these years, too. Besides the recurring epidemics and plagues there was the great fire of 1788. On Good Friday of that year the entire city burned to the ground except for perhaps a half dozen buildings.

Out of the ruins came a new city, much more solid and more beautiful than the one that had been destroyed. The new houses were built of stone instead of wood. There was a new St. Louis Cathedral, much handsomer than the previous one. Erected beside it was the Cabildo, where the Spanish officials had their offices, and which was soon to be called one of the most beautiful buildings in America.

In 1794 there was another large fire, but this did much less damage than the previous one. None of the finest buildings was destroyed. Through all this the city grew and prospered.

Yet although New Orleans welcomed growth and prosperity, and now put up with the Spaniards, it was still a French city — in everything but ownership. As the terrors of the French Revolution faded away Orleanians began to travel to France again. French politics and changes in government aroused their interest more than the affairs of any other nation.

When Napoleon began his rise as a great military leader and won victory after victory for

France over other countries, the citizens of New Orleans looked upon him as their hero, too. He was always to be admired and loved in New Orleans. Its people watched eagerly when he became ruler of France in 1799, with the title of "First Consul." Here, many Orleanians told each other, was a leader who might restore New Orleans and Louisiana to France. Down with Spain! They would be French again.

That is why Thomas Jefferson believed New Orleans to be so dangerous. What would happen to the United States if the city became again a possession of France, especially under the leadership of such a conqueror as Napoleon? What could the United States do if the powerful armies of Napoleon were to appear in the Mississippi River?

Jefferson watched with grave concern.

5: *Napoleon Bonaparte's Wars*

UNTIL 1800 NAPOLEON WAS TOO BUSY WITH other matters to do anything about Louisiana. He had talked of it to his intimates and his advisors, however, and he remembered well that the colony had once been French. He knew, too, that the French people had never forgotten it,

and that it had been named after their beloved
King Louis XIV.

Already one of Napoleon's advisors, the
powerful Talleyrand, had almost brought about
a war between France and the United States. In
1794 Talleyrand had visited the new nation and
had disliked everything he saw. He dreamed of
restoring to France all her lost colonies.

When Jefferson's treaty with Spain in 1797
gave Americans the right to use the Mississippi
River once more, Talleyrand was loud in warning
the French against the United States. He said
all Americans were "devoured by pride and am-
bition." He urged France to regain Lousiana
and the Floridas from Spain. Then these colonies
would be "a wall of brass" between the United
States and England. He was constantly telling
Spain she had nothing to fear from France, that
those nations would always be friends.

Yet Napoleon, no Frenchman, but born on the
island of Corsica and of Italian blood, would one
day be Emperor of France. More than that, he
had dreams of ruling the world. As a first
step toward the fulfillment of his dream, he was
to attempt to regain Louisiana for France.

Napoleon Bonaparte entered the French army

after attending a military school in Paris. He fought well and bravely. Later, however, he found himself in political trouble and was put in prison. After his release he was employed by the War Office, and later re-entered the army. When the Austrians invaded Italy, Napoleon led against them what was known as the Army of Italy.

In June 1798 he led French armies into Egypt in an attempt to conquer that country. He won a great many battles, but his ambitions were ruined when Lord Nelson and the British navy wiped out the French fleet.

In February 1799 Napoleon invaded Syria, but the British defeated him there, too. Returning to Egypt, he defeated the Turks in a great battle in July. In October, he was again in France, where he was created ruler and given his title as "First Consul."

His first action in his new role was to lead a French army across the Alps and win the great victory against the Austrians at Marengo. Then he began planning new conquests. Most of all he wanted to defeat Great Britain, whom he considered the worst enemy of France. Already he dreamed of becoming Emperor of France.

"In two years," he told his brother, Joseph Bonaparte, "we shall be the masters of the world."

At this time France was looked upon almost as an enemy by the United States. While Napoleon was fighting the Battle of Marengo, American representatives, sent by President John Adams, then in office, arrived in Paris.

John Adams was a Federalist, and many of the Federalists, led by Alexander Hamilton, wanted war with France. That country had been seizing American ships and ruining United States commerce. Yet the United States had a treaty with France. By this treaty the United States was supposed to aid France against her enemies, help her defend her colonies in the West Indies, and send her food and supplies. Many Americans, remembering the Revolution and still hating the British were in sympathy with France.

The Federalists, on the other hand, were in sympathy with England. They argued that since the French government had changed hands several times, the treaty between the United States and France no longer existed.

But John Adams, although a Federalist, did not want war with France. He asked only that

France stop seizing American ships and ruining our commerce. The envoys whom he sent to Paris were told to collect $20,000,000 in damages for attacks on American shipping.

When Napoleon returned from Marengo an agreement was reached. The United States would forget the $20,000,000 France owed her. In return France would tear up the treaty that bound the United States to aid her in her wars. The United States government repaid its own citizens the damages due them. It was glad to get rid of the treaty that might have led the country into all of Napoleon's wars.

After that the Federalists were quieter about going to war with France.

In France things were not so quiet. Talleyrand and others in France kept urging Napoleon to get back Louisiana and other French possessions in the Western Hemisphere. It was still going on when Jefferson took John Adams' place as President.

We know that Jefferson had always loved France. He thought of it as his second country, for he had lived there. He had been happy when the people tried to found a republic with democratic laws and freedom, based in some cases on his own beliefs.

But now he had seen many changes in France. What was to have been a democracy had become first a place of bloodshed and terror as heads rolled from the guillotine. Now Napoleon was rising, a tyrant and a dictator.

The United States itself was threatened by France. American ships had been seized and robbed, American lives endangered. Now there was this worry about Louisiana and New Orleans, which Napoleon might get back from Spain at any moment.

Jefferson wrote to Robert Livingston in Paris, in that same letter in which he had described how dangerous New Orleans was to the peace and freedom of the United States:

"The day that France takes possession of New Orleans . . . From that moment we must marry ourselves to the British fleet and nation."

Nothing could better express how desperate Jefferson was. He would join with England, a country he had always disliked, against France, if it were necessary to save the United States. Only a quarter of a century before the United States had won its freedom from Great Britain, but now France had become the young nation's most dangerous enemy. Jefferson knew the government of France had no feelings of friendship toward the United States. He did not think the British did, either, but at the moment they were far less threatening to American freedom.

Jefferson instructed his representatives in France to report to him everything that went on. In Washington he became more friendly with the British representing their country there. Each side watched the other.

In Europe Napoleon worried about the new friendship between the United States and England.

6: *Napoleon and the King of Spain*

IN ORDER TO UNDERSTAND THE STORY OF THE
Louisiana Purchase and how the colony became
a part of the United States we must understand
something about what was going on in Europe
and in other parts of the world. We must understand Napoleon. We must remember that he

was the most important man in Europe at that time.

Nowhere was there a more ambitious man, for he wanted to rule the world. In 1801 it looked as if he might at least rule all Europe as well as many of the far-flung colonies of Europe's nations.

As we know, Louisiana belonged to Spain when Napoleon became the ruler of France. At first he wanted France to regain it. He wanted France to add to her colonies all over the earth, and particularly in the Western Hemisphere. He had been urged in this by Talleyrand and his other advisors.

Yet, Napoleon knew when to place limits to his ambitions. At the time he was neither ready nor anxious to try force against Spain. That did not suit his purposes, for Charles IV, King of Spain and ruler over Spain's tremendous and rich empire, was his friend and his admirer.

The power Napoleon hated and feared most was that of England. France had declared war on England in 1793, just a few days after Louis XVI and Marie Antoinette lost their heads on the guillotine. In 1801 negotiations began on what ultimately was known as the Peace of

Amiens, and for the time being France and England ceased fighting against each other.

It was a peace that was not going to last, but for the time being it, too, suited Napoleon's purposes. Like all dictators he would sign any treaties or papers, or tell any lie that would increase his power or give him a chance to extend his conquests. On the other hand, the British did not take the treaty seriously, either. For a while both waited for the other to make a move.

One thing Napoleon feared was that England and the United States might become allies in a war against France. He knew that many Americans were demanding that Congress declare war on his country. He also knew the United States liked less and less a European power having control over the Mississippi River and the dangerous port of New Orleans.

Still another thing he knew was that Charles IV of Spain placed little value upon Louisiana. The Spanish might not defend New Orleans if the Americans should try to take it.

Charles IV of Spain ruled one of the largest and richest empires of the world during that period, but he does not seem to have been much interested in those parts of it far from home. Actually Spain owned the greater part of the Western Hemisphere. All South America, we must remember, belonged to Spain, as did all of what we now call Central America. Mexico, Texas, the Floridas, and, of course, all Louisiana belonged to Spain. The power and the possessions of Spain stretched from the Canadian border in the Colony of Louisiana to the borders of Patagonia. Her island colonies were strewn through the Caribbean Sea.

But Charles IV seems to have doubted the value of much of his empire. It was costly to maintain and troublesome. The most bothersome of all was Louisiana. The Americans were always intruding this colony, making claims to use of the Mississippi River, and showing that they resented the Spaniards' being there.

Charles IV did not care much for the duties of a king, anyway. He was in many ways a good man and popular with his people. He was very religious and he went to church every day. For a Spanish king he was also extremely democratic. He liked to work with his hands at cabinet-making, at gunsmithery, and at armory. He loved to ride and to hunt and he was said to be the best shot in Europe. Sometimes he shocked the nobles of his court by slapping them on the back and telling them jokes. Every evening he allowed a half hour to his ministers and in this short time all the business of running his empire had to be performed. Most of the time that was left after all these activities, he spent in eating. Charles was a huge eater.

All in all, the King of Spain was not very much like his friend Napoleon, who, in the autumn of 1800, was beginning his attempt to regain Louisiana for France.

The activities of Napoleon were kept as secret as possible and only rumors of what was happening reached the United States. The first step was taken when Talleyrand, at Napoleon's order, sent a courier to the Spanish capital, Madrid. The courier carried an offer to exchange the Duchy of Parma, a part of Italy, which now belonged to France and Napoleon, for Louisiana. The King of Spain's son-in-law, as the Duke of Parma, would rule this territory.

At first the Queen of Spain seems to have been more enthusiastic about this than her husband. She wanted this duchy for her daughter. There were more notes and more negotiations. Sometimes Napoleon threatened. In one dispatch he

warned the King of Spain that the close relation
then existing between the United States and
England "may and must some day bring these
two powers together in concert for the conquest
of the Spanish colonies."

Arguments went on for two years. At first
Napoleon demanded that the Floridas be included in the exchange of territories. This
Charles IV refused. Then Charles IV demanded
that the exact borders of his son-in-law's future
kingdom be outlined. Napoleon promised the
whole North Italian Kingdom of Tuscany.

More and more news of all this reached the
United States. It was slow in coming. It took
months for the American minister in Paris,
Robert Livingston, to get messages across the
the Atlantic Ocean to Washington. It took more
months for the answers to reach him. But
America and Jefferson watched as carefully as
possible.

In the summer of 1801, Pierre du Pont de
Nemours, a Frenchman who had been living in
the United States for several years, returned to
France. Being a friend of Jefferson, he took messages from the President to the French government asking to be informed about what was go-

ing on between France and Spain. De Nemours received no satisfactory answer.

At the same time, many men in the government in Washington and among the American public were becoming more and more excited. The Federalists again demanded that the United States declare war upon France.

Jefferson, always a peace-lover, refused to listen to this. He was called "timid" and a "pacifist." But he preferred using other means than war. He knew such a war might be the worst thing that could happen to the United States at that time. He wrote in a letter that this hour was "the most important the United States has ever met since their independence."

He still did not think the United States could stand against Napoleon and France, the greatest military power in the world. He was not at all sure of aid from England should such a war come. For the moment, England and France were at peace.

So he waited. It was difficult with his enemies within the country attacking him every moment. Yet we know now it was one of the great deeds of Jefferson's life.

At last Napoleon and Charles IV of Spain reached an agreement. In October 1802 France and Spain formally swapped territories. France again owned Louisiana.

Charles IV thought he was the one who had made the best bargain. He had traded a wilderness containing some 50,000 people, most of them wild Indians, for a civilized kingdom of more than one million inhabitants! His own son-in-law and his daughter would rule Tuscany with the titles of King and Queen. He must have thought he had outwitted even the great Napoleon Bonaparte. He could not understand why Napoleon wanted that Louisiana wilderness at all. It was so expensive and so difficult to run.

The Spanish king did not know that this exchange was the beginning of the end of the Spanish empire in the Western Hemisphere. He did not know it was the beginning of the end of Spain as a world power. Napoleon had promised him that France would never part with Louisiana to any other country. Some writers of history think Napoleon had no intention of keeping that promise at all. Others believe that he really did plan to make Louisiana a permanent colony of France when he first made the bargain.

One thing we do know. Napoleon never allowed the son-in-law of Charles IV to rule in Tuscany. The young man had thought he would one day become King of Italy. Instead, when he arrived to take over his Tuscan throne he found the small kingdom still run by the French army and according to Napoleon's laws. So, at least for the time being, Napoleon had Louisiana and he kept Tuscany, too. The new King of Tuscany had only a crown that meant nothing at all.

7: *Robert Livingston in Paris*

THE ACTUAL TRANSFER OF LOUISIANA FROM Spain back to France took place on October 15, 1802. But Napoleon had known long before this that the United States was watching all that was going on between himself and the King of Spain. The American Minister to France, Robert

R. Livingston, had made the interest of the United States in the transaction very plain.

Robert Livingston, as ambassador to France, was the man upon whom Thomas Jefferson had to depend for the protection of American interests in dealing with Napoleon. Livingston was a capable, experienced, and brilliant statesman, with a long career in public life behind him. He was, first of all, an ardent American patriot, whose democratic beliefs and principles were much like Jefferson's. He had been an intimate friend of George Washington, a member of Congress, and a member of the committee that put Jefferson's Declaration of Independence into its final form. He was in every way a good and fortunate choice for his job.

Early in 1801 Livingston informed Jefferson of the rumors that Napoleon had sent a representative to Madrid to ask for the return of Louisiana to France. He continued to keep the President informed as best he could, using the slow communications of the time. At the same time he let his country's opinion reach the ears of the diplomats who supported Napoleon: the United States looked with disfavor upon the return of New Orleans to French control.

A few weeks later Livingston learned that Lucien Bonaparte, one of Napoleon's brothers, had reached a definite decision with Charles IV. Spain and France would definitely exchange territories, although the exact details had yet to be reached, and the actual transfer was not to take place for more than a year.

In September 1801 James Madison, then Secretary of State, and destined to become the next President of the United States, instructed Livingston to obtain more definite information. Livingston was also told to try to buy the Floridas and New Orleans.

Nothing was said about the rest of Louisiana at this time. It was only New Orleans and the Floridas that the United States wanted, and the reason for this is easy to understand. These two territories would give the United States ownership of the mouth of the Mississippi River and control of that part of the Gulf of Mexico and the Caribbean Sea on which they bordered.

Now Livingston tried to reach Napoleon with an offer to purchase this much of the North American continent. It was Talleyrand with whom he had to speak concerning the purchase, but Talleyrand said it was too early for such a discussion. The truth was that France did not yet really own New Orleans or the Floridas.

On November 21, 1801, Rufus King, the American ambassador to London, sent word to Jefferson that he, too, had information that Spain was returning Louisiana to France. This strengthened the suspicions and fears in Washington. And with this came a further rumor even more fearful. It was said that Napoleon intended to use the island of San Domingo in the West Indies as a base of operations. From there he would move through New Orleans to occupy all of Louisiana. (San Domingo is the island now called Haiti.)

This was not entirely a rumor. Napoleon had signed the Peace Treaty of Amiens and for the moment at least he was not at war with England. It was an excellent opportunity for him to occupy Louisiana. He knew he was greatly admired in New Orleans and that its citizens would welcome his rule. He had been informed of this by one of his staunchest supporters, the Baron Joseph de Pontalba, who had lived in New Orleans for some years. The baron also warned him in letters of American interest in the port.

Napoleon knew that England and America

might both go to war against France at this time. It was a danger that he did not relish. Yet he went on with his plans to take over Louisiana. He ordered his Minister of the Navy, Decrès, to organize both military and administrative bodies. It was planned to send French criminals and unemployed persons to the colony. Arms and munitions for an army were prepared.

There were also to be trinkets and other presents for the Indians inhabiting the colony. Each Indian chief was to receive a special medal engraved with the likeness of Napoleon Bonaparte.

When his preparations were completed, the dictator waited for the transfer of Louisiana from Spain. In the meantime his plans were kept as secret as possible, and even most Frenchmen believed the plans concerned an invasion of San Domingo instead of Louisiana.

It was on April 18, 1802, that Jefferson sent Livingston the famous letter, already quoted in part, in which he wrote: "There is on the globe one single spot, the possessor of which is our natural and habitual enemy. It is New Orleans. . . ."

Later he referred to the "common purposes of the United British and American nations."

This was strange talk from Jefferson, who had always hated the English and loved the French, but he had come to realize that there would be nothing else for America to do. She would be forced into an agreement of some kind with the British. This would make the two former enemies—England and the United States—allies against the ambitions of Napoleon.

Yet even then Jefferson did not want war. At the end of the letter he said, "But still we should consider New Orleans and the Floridas as no equivalent for the risk of a quarrel with France. . . ."

In other words, he would not go to war against France even if the French should occupy New Orleans. Only for our own protection would he ally this country with England against actual invasion by Napoleon's armies.

It was during the spring of 1802 that the American people knew with certainty that Louisiana would become Napoleon's property. This news was followed as usual by a great cry among the Federalists and others that Jefferson should declare war against France. Jefferson preferred to find another way.

In the meantime Robert Livingston was still

using every effort to solve the problem in Paris. In his meetings with Talleyrand, Livingston reminded the French statesman of the old and strong friendship between the United States and France. He tried to explain how necessary it was for America to have the port of New Orleans for its commerce. He argued that if New Orleans were a part of the United States it would stand as a barrier between the rest of Louisiana, which would still be a French possession, and any attempted invasion by the British. This would be greatly to the advantage of France should she and England find themselves at war again. In that case, Livingston said, the United States and France would be allies again, as they had in the past.

On the other hand, if Napoleon refused to sell New Orleans, the United States had no choice but to form a partnership with Great Britain. Livingston offered Napoleon $2,000,000 for New Orleans alone.

Talleyrand listened, but the answer was always the same. He would consult the First Consul. Once Talleyrand had been the more powerful, but now Napoleon was the dictator, and Napoleon made all decisions in French affairs.

The situation seemed hopeless to Livingston. He sent Jefferson bleak, discouraging messages: It was useless to go on with the argument; Napoleon's mind could not be reached or changed by anything but his own desires.

And Napoleon was still busy trying to talk Charles IV into giving him the Floridas along with Louisiana. Even after October 15, 1802, when the Spanish King signed the documents in Barcelona that made Louisiana French once more, Napoleon continued his fight for these other territories. Talleyrand advised him against trying to get East Florida. West Florida, which would include the Appalachicola and the port of Pensacola would be enough, he said. By leaving East Florida to Spain, difficulties with the United States might be avoided.

Napoleon ignored this advice. He continued his efforts to get both the Floridas. He offered more Italian territory to the son-in-law of Charles IV. The Spanish Queen urged her husband to consent, but the King, who did listen to his advisors, again refused to part with any more Spanish colonies on the North American continent.

8: *The Closing of the Mississippi*

T HEN THERE OCCURRED AN EVENT THAT AL-
most brought an end to Jefferson's patience.
Louisiana was transferred from Spain to France
on October 15, 1802. On October 16, the very
next day, the port of New Orleans was closed to
American shipping!

Strangely, it was not the French who did this, but the Spanish who were still the rulers of New Orleans and would be for some time to come. Their order to cease what was called "the right to deposit" had come from the man who controlled the customs—Don Juan Ventura Morales, the Spanish Intendant at New Orleans.

Don Morales is said to have been a man "beyond corruption," honest and devoted to Spain's interests. Yet he was a man of narrow mind and prejudices. He was mean and bitter. He hated Americans and the United States. He despised the French.

For a long time he had known of the exchange of land that Napoleon and Charles IV were planning. Now he wanted to do anything and everything he could to hurt both the French and the Americans.

Even the Spanish Governor at New Orleans, Don Juan de Salcedo, disagreed with Morales' action. Salcedo was new in Louisiana, but he was liked by the citizens of New Orleans. He was not fond of Americans, and he had just sent a Spanish militia to guard Natchitoches when he heard a rumor that Americans from across the Mississippi River were threatening to take over that village. Yet he thought Morales was wrong in not allowing the Americans to bring their commerce into New Orleans. It worked a hardship on the citizens of the city themselves, and it caused more trouble in a period already filled with danger and worry.

But even though he was the governor of Louisiana, Salcedo had no power over Morales. Spain ran her colonies in a peculiar way. Each Spanish official was a law unto himself with the exception of obedience to orders from the government at home in Madrid. Salcedo went so far as to threaten Morales with dismissal, but he had no real authority to fire him. The best he could do was to send a letter to Spain stating his objections. He would have to wait until a sailing vessel plowed across the seas to that country and another vessel returned with an answer. That would take a long time.

When the news reached Washington in November there were men in Congress who blamed Napoleon. They said it was a trick and that Morales, through secret orders from Charles IV, was following the wishes of the French tyrant. Although Louisiana was now French, the Spanish authorities would remain in charge of

New Orleans until French officials took over. For this reason it was believed that the Spanish were now obeying French instructions.

This does not seem to have been true. Apparently Morales had made the decision himself. According to the Spanish system of operating the colonies, he had a right to do anything he pleased in regard to running the port.

Morales argued that he was within his rights. Yes! The treaty of 1797 between the United States and Spain had given Americans the right to bring their produce and goods into the New Orleans wharves. However, said Morales, that right was to be given to Americans for three years, and the three years were long past. During this time Spain had not been able to collect any duties.

Morales claimed that, besides the legal merchandise which had been allowed to enter the city, there had been quantities of smuggled goods. He claimed, too, that Spain's treasury was losing a great deal of money by allowing the Americans to use the port without charge.

The Americans answered that Spain had made money from their using New Orleans. Americans did not pay duty, but they paid for the use of storage along the docks.

Morales' ruling meant ruin for the Americans who had been using the port. Flatboats and barges came down the river loaded with cotton, sugar, tobacco, and perishable vegetables. Morales' men along the wharves refused to allow the boats to land and unload. The produce rotted, and bargeloads had to be dumped into the river. Then the weary boatmen—Kentuckians and Tennesseans—turned and started for home again. But some stayed to rage and threaten, as they had done before the days of the treaty.

Angry threats did not frighten Morales. When word reached him that the government in Washington was furious he shrugged his shouldres. What did it matter, he asked. Louisiana was now French. This was not Spain's problem any longer. Let France settle it! He and the other Spanish authorities would remain in New Orleans only until the French took over. In the meantime why should Spain spend money to please Americans? From his viewpoint it made sense. It also gave him a chance to enjoy what he was doing to the Americans he hated.

When the Spanish treasury got word to

Salcedo, asking him to do something about this, Morales still objected. The Spanish government then told him to find another place along the Mississippi where the Americans might deposit their goods. Morales replied reluctantly that he would see what could be arranged, but he did nothing. More and more Americans suffered losses.

As soon as Livingston in Paris learned that the port of New Orleans had been closed he asked Talleyrand for help. He demanded to know what Napoleon would do about the port when France took possession of it. Talleyrand, playing for time, answered only that the French would consider that problem after they occupied New Orleans.

Now there came further demands upon Thomas Jefferson. Many people wanted the United States to send an army to take New Orleans by force. They feared that if the French were able to move a large force into New Orleans, it would be almost impossible to drive them out. New Orleans and all rights to the Mississippi River would be lost to the United States forever. It was believed that France would keep the port closed to Americans, just as Morales had done.

A kind of written petition from the settlers and rivermen was sent to Congress. It read:

"The Mississippi is ours by the law of nature. Our rivers swell its volume, and flow with it to the Gulf of Mexico. Its mouth is the only issue which nature has given to our waters, and we wish to use it for our vessels. No power in the world should deprive us of our rights. If our liberty in this matter is disputed, nothing shall prevent our taking possession of New Orleans, and when we are once masters of it we shall know how to maintain ourselves there. If Congress refuses us effectual protection we will adopt the measures which our safety requires, even if they endanger the peace of the Union and our connection with the other States. No protection, no allegiance."

This was the most startling of all threats! Not only was there danger of war with France. There was danger of civil war within the United States itself!

Jefferson's enemies took full advantage of this. The Federalists reminded him of their old warning that the United States must go to war with France and Napoleon. Now, they said, the country faced a split among its own states. At this time, with the nation less than thirty years old, with its sections so loosely attached to each other, a quarrel among the states might mean the end of the Union.

This was Jefferson's blackest hour. He must have had a vision of the end of his beloved United States, the end of this struggle to found a true democracy. He must have seen all that might happen, that the states might begin fighting among themselves. This experiment in democracy, this union of free and independent states for the preservation of liberty, would come to an end. It would become a continent of numerous small countries, like Europe. There would be endless wars like the endless wars of Europe.

9: *The Mission of James Monroe*

Yᴇᴛ, ᴅᴇꜱᴘɪᴛᴇ ᴛʜᴇ ᴘᴏꜱꜱɪʙɪʟɪᴛʏ ᴏꜰ ᴛʜɪꜱ dreadful end for the United States, Jefferson never thought it would really happen. For one thing, these "Westerners," as the men of Kentucky and Tennessee were called then, were among Jefferson's staunchest supporters. He believed they would give their President a fair trial.

He still believed a foreign war would be a disaster for the nation, but he knew French troops in New Orleans might mean such a war could not be prevented. Warnings came from all over the southern section of the country.

William Charles Cole Claiborne, then the governor of what was called the "Mississippi Territory," sent messages from Natchez. He would, said Claiborne, be powerless if Napoleon's army should occupy New Orleans and then move toward the Mississippi Territory.

In the town of Frankfort, Kentucky, a newspaper, the *Palladium,* published the statement that "The Kentuckymen have often wished for an opportunity to sack New Orleans, and the day may not be too far distant." Jefferson did not need this warning. He already knew the needs of those Americans who depended upon the Mississippi River and New Orleans. He knew, too, that they would be driven to desperate means if they continued to be deprived of making a living through their commerce.

In Paris, Robert Livingston was having no luck with the French officials. There was no word from Napoleon.

Napoleon's representatives were still busy working out the details of the agreements between Spain and France. Napoleon continued to insist that France must have the Floridas, or at least West Florida. Charles IV refused. The King of Spain would not have cared, but the strongest of his advisors, Don Manual Godoy, known in Spain as the "Prince of Peace," kept Charles IV from giving any part of the Floridas away.

Jefferson's next move was through the Spanish ambassador in Washington, Don Carlos Martinez de Yrujo. Yrujo was a close friend of Jefferson. This young, stubborn, and fearless Spaniard had been in the United States for a number of years. In that time he seems to have become very American in thought and feeling, and to have developed a great fondness for the United States. He had an American wife, the daughter of Governor McKean of Pennsylvania.

Yrujo was devoted to Spain, his country, and to his king, Charles IV. However, he always said what he thought, and he had no fear of royalty or of dictators. He despised Napoleon.

It was Yrujo who told Jefferson that the closing of the port at New Orleans was not the result of an order given by the King of Spain. In a hot and angry letter to Morales, Yrujo accused him of overstepping his rights in closing New Orleans to American commerce. He warned him that Spain might have to repay the Americans who had lost so much money because of this action. But for the moment nothing changed.

When Congress met in December 1802 the city of Washington throbbed with excitement. Yet when Jefferson addressed the Congress there was much disappointment among those who still wanted war with France. Jefferson spoke of many matters before he mentioned New Orleans and Louisiana. He spoke of treaties with the Indians, of the blockade of Tripoli by the Barbary pirates, of taxes, debts, and the needs of the navy. Only at the end did he refer to the subject that was now the most important in the country. He said that the gift of Louisiana to France would change the whole foreign policy of the United States. He did not mention the closing of New Orleans at all.

Afterwards Jefferson explained that he did this on purpose. He was playing for time. He was making plans, but he was not yet ready to tell them. His enemies in Congress attacked him again, but Jefferson paid them little attention.

The "western" states of Kentucky and Tennessee again demanded that the United States seize New Orleans. They urged that this country declare war on France the moment French troops and ships appeared at the mouth of the Mississippi River.

Once more Jefferson talked the "Westerners" into giving him time. Early in January 1803 he took the first step in his new plans. He wrote to James Monroe and asked him to go to Paris.

James Monroe was then the Governor of Virginia. He was a lifelong friend of Thomas Jefferson under whom he had studied law. Monroe had fought in the Revolution as a lieutenant. He had represented Virginia in the approving of the Constitution by the Congress in 1788. A few years after that he had been Ambassador to France. As we know, he was to become the fifth President of the United States.

Jefferson could not have picked a better man to help solve this country's problems, for Monroe was popular in Washington and throughout the country. Actually Jefferson felt that Robert Livingston could do as much with Napoleon as anyone else, but he knew the sending of Monroe would quiet the restlessness among the states.

After Jefferson received the consent of Congress to this appointment, Monroe went to Washington for instructions. Under the title of Minister Extraordinary, he was to join Livingston in Paris and work with him in both Paris and Spain. His particular task was to try to buy New Orleans and West Florida, but he was to offer no more than two or three million dollars. Nothing was said about the rest of Louisiana. It was still only the Mississippi River and the ports along the Gulf of Mexico that interested the government at Washington and the people of the United States.

But as usual in those days things moved slowly. January and February passed before Monroe sailed. There was more argument in Congress and among Jefferson's advisors. At last it was decided that Monroe might offer as much as ten million dollars for New Orleans and West Florida. If this was refused Monroe was to get permission for the United States to build another port on the Mississippi River opposite New Orleans, which Americans could use for the shipping of their goods.

Later Jefferson was to explain all this. He did

not think either Livingston or Monroe could persuade Napoleon to sell New Orleans to the United States. He expected New Orleans to be occupied by Napoleon's army. He did think that some day the city would be owned by the United States, but not before war broke out again between France and Great Britain.

Jefferson warned Congress that the United States must build up her military forces. American troops must be sent to occupy the country along the eastern banks of the Mississippi River. Then, at the right moment, the United States would join Great Britain in driving the French out of New Orleans. In this event, the President believed, the United States would be able to claim New Orleans as its own. That was why he kept working to hold off a war. It was proof of his genius as a statesman.

A public dinner was held for James Monroe early in March. A toast was given to the new Minister Extraordinary, "Peace, if peace is honorable; war, if war is necessary!" That said everything there was to say about the position of the United States.

At last, on March 8, 1803, James Monroe sailed for France. He could not have started out with much hope in his heart. All the messages from Livingston continued to be discouraging. The news from the Americans trying to unload their goods at New Orleans was as bad as ever. The only good report was that most Americans, and particularly those of Kentucky and Tennessee, had quieted a little. They had faith in Monroe and they seemed willing to wait and see what he could do.

Jefferson's hope was to keep peace as long as possible. At least the French had not yet occupied New Orleans. Napoleon's troops, although organized, had not yet set sail. Even now time was on the side of the United States. Jefferson began plans for a fleet of gunboats to navigate the Mississippi River. If the United States had a chance to make itself strong enough there would be no war. Soon American gunboats would patrol the Mississippi and an American army would be on guard on the eastern shore of the river. At the sight of such strength, any nation—French or Spanish—would fear keeping the port of New Orleans closed against Americans.

Jefferson went on, building up American strength, but still the French fleet did not arrive at New Orleans. Jefferson knew what had happened. Napoleon was having trouble on the Caribbean island of San Domingo, and that was where he needed his resources.

10: *The Black Napoleon*

T HIS IS NOT THE PLACE TO TELL THE WHOLE
story of what was going on down in San Domingo. That would take a book all by itself. But it
played such an important part in the Louisiana
Purchase that some of it must be told. For if
there had not been trouble in San Domingo the

Louisiana Territory might not have become American for a long time to come.

San Domingo was the island that we now call Haiti. It is one of the West Indies that lie in the warm water of the Caribbean Sea. Today half of the island is occupied by the Republic of Haiti, the other half by the Dominican Republic. In the days of Jefferson and Napoleon it was also divided into two sections. The larger part belonged to Spain, the other part to France. The French part, in a roughly defined way, became the Republic of Haiti.

At the time that Monroe sailed for France there was a little revolution going on in Haiti. Small as it was, it was giving Napoleon Bonaparte his largest headache.

Before the French Revolution in 1789 the French part of the island of San Domingo had been the most valuable of all of the far-flung colonies of France. It supplied France with sugar, indigo, coffee, and cotton worth a million and a half dollars a year. Seven hundred French ships plowed the seas between France and this tiny island, bearing the produce of San Domingo to French markets. It has been said that two-thirds of the wealth of France came from French San Domingo.

The island had about six hundred thousand inhabitants. Only about fifty thousand of these were white colonists from France. Five hundred thousand were Negro slaves, who were badly treated, worked hard, and lived in poverty and misery. The rest were what were called "free people of color"—persons who had Negro blood, but were free and sometimes prosperous and educated.

There is not space for details here, but the first demand for freedom began when news of the French Revolution reached the island. At first there was trouble only between the French on the island and the "free people of color." Then, on an August night in 1791, the five hundred thousand Negro slaves revolted. Whites and "free people of color" were massacred, cities and towns were set on fire, blood drenched the island. The white people who escaped—and they were few— boarded ships for New Orleans. All the others were killed with barbarous brutality. Many of these Negroes were fresh from Africa, savages who had been made more cruel than ever by the harsh treatment of their owners.

France was busy with her revolution and there was little that could be done. Spain sent troops in from her side of the island, but this did little good. For several years the Negro slaves were alone in French San Domingo. Then, in 1794, the French government gave power over the island to a Negro chief named Toussaint L'Ouverture. Two years later he was given the title of General-in-Chief. Soon he had absolute power over the colony.

Toussaint, the son of a Negro chieftain, had been born on the slave coast of Africa and he had been brought to San Domingo as a slave. He had no education, but he was intelligent, shrewd, and ambitious. He ruled his people with an iron hand, but he did what he could to help them and he dreamed of complete freedom from France.

When France sent representatives to the island Toussaint L'Ouverture treated them well. The principal of these, a man named Roume, found, however, that although he had been sent out to give Toussaint instructions, he was taking orders from Toussaint. Yet no real trouble began until France installed a mulatto, named Rigaud, in command of the southern portion of the island. Toussaint determined to rid himself of Rigaud.

Toussaint had not always been friendly to the United States. His ships had raided American vessels in the first years of his coming into power. But in 1789 he had sent a representative to President John Adams in Washington and completed a treaty with the United States by which he was to send the island's produce to this country in exchange for military supplies. All this was done without asking the permission of the French Republic.

Then Toussaint attacked Rigaud and drove him out of the country. A few days later he threw Roume, the French representative, into prison. A few weeks later, leading his hastily organized troops of former slaves, he seized the Spanish part of the island. Now all the island of San Domingo was his.

Napoleon was furious, but for the moment he could do nothing. It was 1800. He was still at war with England. He sent Toussaint angry threats. Toussaint replied with defiance. He increased his army. He announced that San Domingo was now a republic and would rule itself. Napoleon was indignant and angry. Did this son of an African chief imagine he could defy the legions of France? Napoleon hated the word "republic" anyway.

But what made him angrier than anything else was the way Toussaint imitated him. He called himself the "Black Napoleon" and the "Napoleon of the Antilles." He wore a Napoleonic hat and strutted and posed. He refused to deal with any persons of lesser rank than kings and presidents. In many other ways he acted like Napoleon himself. Soon all Europe was laughing at this; and Napoleon could stand anything but being laughed at. Toussaint became the man whom the dictator hated more than any other in the world. He vowed that Toussaint must be destroyed at any cost. He had no idea what it *was* going to cost.

In October 1801 a great French fleet was ready to sail for San Domingo. At its head was Captain-General Charles Leclerc, who was married to Napoleon's young sister, Pauline. The fleet was a huge one, with ten thousand men aboard its vessels. This, thought Napoleon, would surely mean the end of the Republic of San Domingo and Toussaint L'Ouverture.

The fleet arrived in sight of the island in January 1802. Toussaint saw it approach from a lookout in the mountains. By his side was Henri Christophe, a young Negro aide. Toussaint sent Christophe to take command of the town of Cap Français. On February 5, as Leclerc and his men attacked the town, Christophe set Cap Français on fire. Once a beautiful city, most of it burned to ashes.

The Negroes retreated to the hills and mountains, and this stage of the fighting went on for three months. Leclerc's army drove forward into the island, but Toussaint's people knew the country; the Frenchmen did not. The Black Napoleon ordered town after town to be set to the torch.

The anger of Charles Victor Emmanuel Leclerc grew as weeks and months passed and Toussaint and his army still refused to surrender. The French won every battle, but the cost was bitter. Leclerc lost thousands of men—and his temper. How dare these savages fight against the army of France, the army of Napoleon!

Now further instructions came from Napoleon. Leclerc was to try to bring about peace. He was to offer the Negroes freedom if Toussaint would surrender. He was to promise they would never be slaves again. A full set of new laws was sent, not to Toussaint, but to Henri Christophe. Christophe was to persuade Toussaint to accept the offers of the French.

Christophe accepted and, at last, so did Toussaint. Toussaint made the fatal mistake of trusting Napoleon. In a way it was Christophe, himself ambitious to rule San Domingo, who betrayed Toussaint. Toussaint believed Christophe. He believed Leclerc, who gave him his word of honor that Toussaint would be made a general in the French army again and that his people would be free.

In May, three months after the fighting had begun, the island was quiet. Toussaint rode into Leclerc's camp. At first he was received with honor. But in June he was arrested and taken aboard a French ship. No one on San Domingo ever saw the Black Napoleon again. He died a year later in a prison in France.

A few days after the arrest of Toussaint a new order came from Napoleon. The people of San Domingo were to be returned to slavery!

It was easy to give such an order, but Leclerc soon found it impossible to follow. His army began trying to round up the Negroes. There was immediate revolt and terrible fighting. It went on all summer. Driven mad by the news that they were to be slaves again, the Negroes killed and killed, without regard for their own lives. By September 1802 Leclerc had lost seventeen thousand men.

Even when captured the Negroes preferred to die rather than be slaves again. In one case 176 were taken prisoner and locked up in a stockade. By morning 173 had committed suicide by strangling themselves.

Then, early in September, yellow fever broke out among the men of the new army Napoleon had sent to fight under Leclerc. Before the month was over four thousand Frenchmen had died of the disease. The Negroes, used to the climate and its diseases, were not affected.

This was the real beginning of the disaster of San Domingo so far as Napoleon was concerned. On September 16, 1802 Leclerc wrote Napoleon that almost twenty-four thousand Frenchmen had died on San Domingo since he had arrived to take charge.

On October 7 Leclerc wrote the First Consul of a new plan. He intended to kill every Negro on the island except those under twelve years of age. A month later, before this plan was begun, Leclerc died of yellow fever.

This was just after the transfer of Louisiana from Spain to France. Napoleon was organizing a force to occupy New Orleans, and having medals engraved for the Indian chiefs. Now all these preparations stood still.

The dictator was in a rage. He knew he must conquer San Domingo before he could send his army to Louisiana. He was conquering Europe, he believed it was his destiny to rule the world, but he could not conquer the little island inhabited by slaves. For all his genius he did not know that people who are enslaved will fight more fiercely for freedom than any other people.

By the spring of 1803, when James Monroe was sailing for Paris, fifty thousand Frenchmen had died on San Domingo. Back in the mountains Henri Christophe had become the leader of the people in place of Toussaint.

Napoleon was never to conquer the island. In a way it was his greatest defeat.

So it was the fighting on San Domingo upon which Jefferson counted for time. He believed, correctly, that Napoleon would not try to occupy Louisiana until he had recaptured the island.

And he believed San Domingo would go on fighting for a long time. Every day that Napoleon's armies were kept out of New Orleans gave him new hope that the United States might be able to buy the port.

11: *The Price of Empire*

NAPOLEON HAD MANY PROBLEMS IN THE spring of 1803. The death of Leclerc on San Domingo had been a great blow. True, Toussaint had been captured and was even then dying in a French prison, but this brought the conquest of San Domingo no closer.

The fleet and the army that were to have occupied New Orleans still waited. Napoleon feared he might have to use this force against San Domingo, too.

One of the weakest links in the armor of France was her navy. Napoleon did not have a large navy to spare for colonial conquest. He could not spare ships for both Louisiana and San Domingo. Moreover, his San Domingo armies were grumbling. Frenchmen dreaded being sent to the island, for they feared the fever far more than fighting.

Napoleon had many troubles at home, too. He needed money. He had been forced to abandon his conquest of Egypt for the time being. He had given up Corsica. He knew the peace between France and England could not last. Signs of its end were already in sight.

To make up for his losses of Egypt and Corsica, Napoleon needed to conquer Malta. This island in the Mediterranean was at that time occupied by the British. During a meeting with the British ambassador to France, Lord Whitworth, Napoleon even made a threat. "I must have either Malta or war!" he told the Englishman.

Robert Livingston was present at that scene and he described it in a letter to James Madison, the Secretary of State in Washington. It seemed to him that war between France and England was about to begin again, and of course he was right.

Nor was Napoleon any longer satisfied with his position as First Consul of France. He wanted to be Emperor. He was to give himself that crown and title in another year, but to win it he needed new victories, new conquests. Yet he was already learning something about the price of empire. Several attempts had already been made upon his life by his enemies, most of them royalists who dreamed of restoring the old line of the kings of France.

But for more than any other reason Napoleon needed war in Europe to make people forget San Domingo and his dismal failure there. To begin this war—and England was to be the nation he preferred attacking first—he needed money.

He had sent General Rochambeau to take the place of Leclerc on San Domingo. By a curious coincidence, Rochambeau had fought at George

Washington's side at Yorktown and had aided in
the capture of Cornwallis. He was a seasoned
warrior and no stranger to the Western Hemisphere, but he had no more success at San
Domingo than had the younger and less experienced Leclerc. As soon as he arrived on the
island Rochambeau dispatched a message to
Napoleon, announcing that only an army of
thirty-five thousand new men could win the
struggle against Christophe.

Napoleon brooded about this. Did he dare to
give up San Domingo entirely? It was about this
time that Napoleon began to stand entirely alone,
to plan and scheme without consulting any of
his advisors. No one knows exactly what went on
in his mind just then, but we do know that he
decided his destiny lay in Europe, not in the
Western Hemisphere. If the colonies must go,
let them go. He could not afford to pour out all
his strength, his men and money, to win back
San Domingo, to occupy Louisiana. He did not
have enough to spread that thinly. If he made
war on England, as he planned to do, and if he
should be defeated, it would be the end of Napoleon himself.

But he made the promises expected of him. He told Rochambeau that he was preparing to send fifteen thousand men to San Domingo immediately, and that he would send another fifteen thousand later on. At a meeting with Godoy, who represented the King of Spain, Napoleon promised that he would never part with Louisiana. Should the need for doing so ever come, he assured Godoy, he would return the colony to Spain before letting any other country have it.

So Spain was contented for the moment, and down in San Domingo the fighting went on, becoming worse all the time. A brave and patriotic soldier, General Rochambeau turned out to be a poor administrator. He wasted money and he was unable to keep his own men obedient to the laws. Moreover, he made no progress toward bringing the bloodshed to an end. Whites and Negroes killed each other on sight. Fevers continued to take more and more French lives.

Napoleon, reading the dispatches, said nothing but he knew he must give up San Domingo. It was a bottomless pit into which he was pouring France herself.

While all this was still going on, Toussaint

died of pneumonia in his French prison. He never knew his people were defeating Napoleon and France.

And Pierre Clement de Laussat, the French Colonial Prefect, or High Commissioner, arrived in New Orleans.

12: *Under Two Flags*

THE SHIPS CARRYING LAUSSAT TO NEW OR-
leans and James Monroe to France might have
passed each other on the high seas. Laussat sailed
for the capital of Louisiana on January 10, 1803,
apparently believing that he was going to New
Orleans to take charge of Louisiana for
Napoleon.

Laussat, an ardent supporter of Napoleon, was honest and intelligent, but he had never traveled, and apparently he had no idea what lay before him. Later he wrote that he had never even seen a sailing ship before he boarded the *Surveillant*. He was so new to the ways of the sea that at one port he almost fell off the gangplank when attempting to go ashore. During most of the trip he was seasick and miserable.

With Laussat traveled his wife, his three young daughters, and his staff, which included a doctor and a General Burthe. By the time the ship reached New Orleans Laussat and the general were already having furious arguments.

These began when the general said, "I shall have charge of the officers and troops when they arrive, and you of the supplies."

To this Laussat replied, "You will have charge of nothing, except under my orders!"

Both men believed that ships bearing French troops would follow them to New Orleans. Laussat meant to be in command of the entire situation.

The *Surveillant* reached the mouth of the Mississippi River on March 11, but the winds were extremely bad and the ship was unable to proceed upstream for days. It was four o'clock in the afternoon of March 26 when she finally arrived at the New Orleans wharves. Cannon were fired in salute and Laussat and his staff were taken to the palace of Spanish Governor de Salcedo at once.

At first everyone treated Laussat like an arriving king. For a home, he and his wife were given one of the finest mansions in the city. They were supplied with furniture, silver, linens, and slaves. Laussat was delighted to hear French spoken all about him, and to listen to constant praise of Napoleon. Even Morales, the customs official who had closed the port against Americans, was polite. The others did everything to make the French Colonial Prefect comfortable.

Laussat had expected that it would be a little while before the Spaniards left the city, giving him full charge. Everything moved slowly at that period, and he was content to wait. Meanwhile, he was happy at finding himself so welcomed, so well treated. He had no suspicion that he did not understand New Orleans at all.

He made his first mistake on his second day in the city. On the morning of that day, March 27, he made his first public speech, standing on the balcony of a building that overlooked the old Place d'Armes. The street below and the square were filled with the curious, mixed population of the town.

Laussat welcomed the people back to French rule. He said, "Your separation from France, the result of a shameful peace following an ignominious war, marks one of the most disgraceful epochs of a weak and corrupted government."

Now there were royalists in New Orleans, people who had been loyal to the French kings. They did not like having Louis XV and Louis XVI called "disgraceful," "weak," and "corrupt." Thus these persons turned against Laussat at once.

In the same speech Laussat made a second mistake. He referred to O'Reilly's brutality, although he tried to please the Spanish at the same time. He said that O'Reilly had been "an agent unworthy of this noble nation."

That afternoon Governor Salcedo took the Frenchman driving in the outskirts of the city and told him he had not been pleased with his words about O'Reilly. It was only then that Laussat realized how many different points of view existed in New Orleans and how many different kinds of people he had to please.

As the days and weeks passed, he did try more and more to please. He was invited everywhere and he entertained the various groups that made up the population of the city. At every opportunity he praised the beauty of the women, the intelligence of the men, the food, the fine manners and elegance for which the town was noted. Most of all he tried to understand the people.

The truth of the matter was that a great many Orleanians had changed their minds during the year that had passed. When they had heard the spring before that New Orleans would be French again, many had been overjoyed; but the winds of feeling had begun to shift.

Of course there were still many enthusiastic admirers of Napoleon in the city. These were as glad as ever about the change. But fear had overtaken other people. Many were talking about San Domingo. Refugees from the island had brought tales of horror with them. The Negroes of New Orleans were terrified at the idea of the French taking over the city. Their white owners had secret fears of a slave-uprising that might bring with it as much bloodshed as the struggle in San Domingo.

Also, there were people who thought changing back to French laws and money and government would be just too much trouble. The Orleanians were pleasure-loving, somewhat lazy, and in many cases indifferent to government and politics. They had become used to Spanish law and Spanish ways of doing government business. It would be a nuisance to change. They did not want to be bothered.

So poor Laussat's happiness soon began to fade. Except for the ardent admirers of Napoleon he could please nobody. His worst enemy turned out to be General Burthe, who had come over on the ship with him. Having no authority himself, he did everything possible to hurt Laussat. He gossiped about him behind his back and did anything he could to make Laussat unpopular. To make matters worse, no troops arrived from France. There was nothing for Laussat to do but wait, while the Spanish continued to run the city and the colony.

His worst blow came on May 10, when the Marquis de Caso Calvo arrived fom Cuba, with the title of Commissioner of the King of Spain. This man was to help Governor Salcedo in the duties of transferring Louisiana to France.

Caso Calvo was haughty, cold, and cruel. His niece had married "Bloody O'Reilly's" son. Of course he was told of Laussat's speech at once. He himself had been in New Orleans with O'Reilly, and had been his admirer. He could not forgive Laussat.

As time passed, the people of New Orleans began to doubt that the colony had really been given back to France. Most of them decided they had better be nice to the Spanish authorities after all. So they deserted Laussat. Before he had been in New Orleans three months the Frenchman who had been received with cannon salutes and treated like royalty found himself alone, isolated, and laughed at. To add to his troubles, he caught yellow fever and almost died.

In the midst of all this there was another event which did not please Laussat either. In April word came from the King of Spain ordering Morales to open the port of New Orleans to American shipping. The Spanish ambassador had at last won this victory with his king. Morales had to obey, so the port was opened. American ships came down the river by the dozen, and Americans poured into New Orleans.

This added to Laussat's anger. At one time he saw fifty-five American ships at the wharves, while there were only ten that were Spanish or French. Too, the Americans who came ashore acted as if they owned New Orleans. Laussat disliked and resented them. In private he swore that if ever he had authority to run the port they would not be allowed to act as they did.

Laussat had a long list of grievances against the Americans. They talked openly of the day when New Orleans would belong to the United States. They boasted of invading the city if they could get it in no other way. They ignored both the Spanish and French administrations. They sang American songs in the streets. Worst of all, they ignored him—Laussat—and to an even greater degree than did the Spanish.

Laussat kept writing to France, in an effort to learn how his government planned to handle his position in New Orleans. He seldom received a reply, so he didn't know what action he was expected to take.

Little as Laussat knew about what was going to happen, the people knew less. What was to become of them? Were they going to live under the Spanish flag or the French flag? No one knew. To Laussat there was something even more discouraging: No one seemed to care very much.

13: *A Time of Indecision*

IF NEW ORLEANS WAS CONFUSED ABOUT WHAT was going to happen to Louisiana it was not alone. Washington wondered, too. So did Paris.

After James Monroe sailed for France there was little to do in Washington but wait. Thomas Jefferson knew this must be America's last chance to buy Louisiana, for war between England and France might break out again at any moment. There were rumors that the English were preparing for this. It was said that one of their first acts would be to send a fleet up the Mississippi River and take New Orleans.

Jefferson knew that there was little choice between France and England as masters of Louisiana. If Napoleon kept the colony the new commissioner, Laussat, was almost sure to close the port as soon as he was placed in full charge of the city. If England invaded New Orleans and claimed it as a prize in a new war with France the port might be closed by the British for some time to come.

The best the United States could hope for at this time was that Napoleon would be willing to sell New Orleans after all. Then the British would not invade it. They did not really want New Orleans, nor did they want a new war with the United States. They would occupy the port only as a blow against France.

All this time the French army, under the command of General Victor, waited in a port of Holland for their orders to sail for Louisiana. Several times Napoleon gave an order and then canceled it, as if he could not make up his mind. Decrès, Minister of the French Navy, urged that the force of occupation depart, but still the First Consul hesitated.

It was a time filled with suspense for Jefferson, and it is fortunate for the history of the United States that he was a patient man and a wise statesman.

England was watching, too. On March 8, 1803, a day when Monroe was on his way to Paris and Laussat on his way to New Orleans, the King of England said in an address to Parliament:

"I am informed of extensive preparations which are being made in the ports of Holland and France, and though I am informed that their objective is the French colonies, I have been obliged to take precautions for the safety of my dominions, the honor of my crown and the interests of my people."

It seemed certain to those who heard the King's speech that war would break out between France and England the moment Napoleon's fleet departed for Louisiana.

A few weeks later Rufus King, the American ambassador to London, was invited to attend a meeting of the English cabinet. Now came a definite offer. The English cabinet told Rufus King that England was willing to seize New Orleans at once and give it to the United States. King promised to dispatch this news to Jefferson and the American government, and informed the English cabinet that Monroe was on his way to France to try to buy New Orleans and the Floridas from Napoleon.

There was still talk of buying the Floridas. Thomas Pinckney, the American ambassador to Spain, had informed Jefferson that Spain had not given France the Floridas along with Louisiana, so now Pinckney was attempting to buy the Floridas from Spain. That, however, already seemed hopeless. Godoy, the Prince of Peace, urged Charles IV not to part with those territories.

Yet all this time, or most of it, Napoleon was playing a game. It was a game which he shared with no one for the moment. The truth was he had no intention of sending an expedition to Louisiana at all.

Napoleon knew that New Orleans was lost. Either England or the United States would have it. He could not hold the port against either country. If he tried he would be at war with both, and he was not prepared for that.

He knew now that France could not hold her distant colonies. San Domingo had been proof of that. France's navy was too weak. Napoleon would not risk fighting England at sea. If he fought her it must be on land, preferably the earth of Europe, for Napoleon was a soldier before anything else. He believed he could lead any army to victory and he believed that with himself in command it was his destiny to win any battle. He was always talking of his "star," and he had firm faith his star directed him to land conquests.

"You must know," he once told his brother, Lucien, "that I have not the slightest intention of fighting England on the open sea because there I should not be in a position to assume personal command; and while I have great faith in French valor, the equal faith that I have in my own lucky star, if not in myself, ordains that I can only count definitely upon victory when I myself am in command."

Actually, Napoleon's faith was only in Napoleon.

Thus, before James Monroe reached the shores

of France Napoleon had already decided to give up Louisiana, and he had decided to see that it went to the United States, not to England. His deep hatred of Great Britain was probably his chief reason for doing this.

Again, by handing Louisiana over to the United States Napoleon would insure friendship between that country and France for a long time to come. He felt this was desirable, for his genius seems to have made it possible for him to see far into the future. One day, he told those around him, the United States would be the most powerful nation in the world. One day she would have a navy stronger and larger than Britain's own. We have seen that come true.

For a while Napoleon said nothing about his intention to sell Louisiana. He knew that not all his ministers and advisors would agree with him. There was also his promise, given to Charles IV of Spain, that he would never part with the colony. However, such promises never kept the dictator from doing as he pleased.

There was another matter even more important to Napoleon: How much money could he get for the colony from the United States? He needed money, although this was not his main reason for selling Louisiana. Some historians have believed that Spain, desiring to restore the colony to the Spanish empire, would have paid him more than he eventually received from the American government. This is probably true, for Godoy had warned the King of Spain that if America ever came into ownership of New Orleans, Spain would find it hard to keep the Floridas. In this, as we know, Godoy was right.

Without a doubt the desire to weaken Spain played a part in Napoleon's scheming. Later he admitted that he hoped the United States and Spain would go to war over the Floridas some day. In all the plans of Napoleon there were hidden tricks. He always wanted to bring about trouble between the nations of the earth so that he might profit by any that were weakened by war.

Therefore, to injure England, to save the strength of his armies in Europe, to make some money for his future wars, possibly to bring about a war between the United States and Spain, Napoleon had made up his mind to sell Louisiana to the United States. The greatest moment in all American history since the Revolution had arrived.

14: Napoleon Takes a Bath

SO BEFORE JAMES MONROE ARRIVED IN PARIS
on April 13, 1803 the decision had been made.
Napoleon seems not to have kept his secret too
long. Once he had made up his mind he always
moved fast.

He first told Talleyrand, who was not pleased,

and who argued with the First Consul. Talleyrand's power was fading now, however, and his opinion had no effect on Napoleon. At last Talleyrand admitted that Louisiana would be difficult for France to hold against either England or America, and that its loss would not destroy the dictator's dreams of empire.

Napoleon next revealed his plan to Barbé Marbois, his Minister of Finance. In Marbois' *History of Louisiana* he quotes the exact words of Napoleon. In part Napoleon said:

"I renounce Louisiana. It is not only New Orleans that I cede; it is the whole colony, without reserve. I know the price of what I abandon. I have proved the importance I attach to this province, since my first diplomatic act with Spain had the object of recovering it. I renounce it with the greatest regret; to attempt obstinately to retain it would be folly. I direct you to negotiate the affair. Have an interview this very day with Mr. Livingston."

That kind of speech was typical of Napoleon. He was always a showman, always theatrical, always performing as if he were on a stage.

Unlike Talleyrand, Marbois agreed with the decision. As a matter of fact, Marbois was fond of the United States. He had lived in this country and he had an American wife. He had very democratic ideas. He did remind Napoleon of his promise to Spain that Louisiana would never be given to any other country. He also reminded him that the actual transfer of the colony to France had not even taken place yet. Laussat was still waiting in New Orleans for that event. All the papers had been signed long ago, but Spanish officials still ruled Louisiana. Napoleon shrugged. That did not matter.

But it was Talleyrand, not Marbois, who broke the news to Robert Livingston. Somehow Talleyrand got there first, perhaps in an attempt to restore himself to Napoleon's favor. Talleyrand asked the American ambassador if the United States would like to buy the whole of Louisiana.

Livingston's reply was "No!" The United States was interested only in purchasing New Orleans and the Floridas.

Actually Livingston was almost knocked off his feet by the sudden offer. In his attempts to buy New Orleans, he had worked so long and argued so long with this very man, Talleyrand, that at first the change of mind was almost too much for Livingston to take. But he continued to tell Talleyrand that the United States did not want all Louisiana!

There had never been any discussion between any members of the government about buying the whole colony. The idea seemed wild and fantastic. Most Americans would have been violently opposed to such a thing if the matter had ever come up. What would the United States do with all that wilderness?

Yet now Livingston began to consider the idea. Anyway, he thought, if that was the only way the United States could get New Orleans, there might be no choice but to accept it all. He made a first offer of two million dollars. Talleyrand refused. That was too low. Livingston answered that Mr. Monroe would be in Paris in a few days and asked for time to discuss the matter with him. Talleyrand agreed.

When Monroe arrived he and Livingston spent the first day talking of Napoleon's offer. At dinner that evening at Livingston's house Marbois joined them for coffee, and Livingston questioned him.

Marbois told Monroe and Livingston he knew a little about Napoleon's decision to sell the colony, but more than that he would not admit.

However, he asked Livingston to come to his house after Monroe had left.

Livingston agreed, and he and Marbois talked almost until morning. During this conversation the purchase of Louisiana by the United States may almost be said to have been decided. No papers were signed and the price was still not settled. Livingston could not close the sale without the authority of the United States government, but he knew now that all Louisiana would soon be American territory.

When he reached home he at once wrote James Madison, the Secretary of State, suggesting strongly that the United States buy the entire territory. Later in the day Livingston told Monroe of his talk with Marbois.

A week was spent deciding the price the United States would pay. The final price decided upon was fifteen million dollars. Yet Monroe and Livingston still hesitated. They had been told they could pay ten million dollars for New Orleans alone, but they could not make up their minds at once to give the extra five million for all the rest of the colony. We must remember that most people thought all of it except New Orleans and the Mississippi River not only worth little, but a burden upon whatever country owned it. It would have to be governed and protected.

As time passed Napoleon grew impatient. There were at least two reasons for this. One was that he wanted the sale completed before Spain heard of it. Another was that many persons close to him were against it. Perhaps the most extreme opponents of the plan were his brothers, Lucien and Joseph.

Napoleon was taking a bath when his brothers came to see him, burning with anger because they had just heard of his intention of selling Louisiana to the United States. Lucien Bonaparte later wrote the story of the scene himself, and put down what we can suppose were the exact words that took place between the three Bonapartes.

Joseph had heard it first and rushed to Lucien's home. Lucien was dressing to go to the theater. "This is no time for theater-going," Joseph cried; "I have news for you that will give you no fancy amusement. The General wants to sell Louisiana." Napoleon's brothers always called him "the General" among themselves. They often used the nickname with scorn. Probably they were jealous of him.

Lucien replied to Joseph that Napoleon would not dare sell Louisiana without the consent of the Chambers. The Chambers was the governing body of France, as is our Congress in this country.

"He means to do it without their consent," was Joseph's reply. "This is what he answered me, when I said to him, as you do, that the Chambers would not consent. What is more, he added that this sale would supply him with funds to pursue the war. Do you know that I am beginning to think he is much too fond of war?"

They went to call upon their brother the next morning. The great Napoleon was in the bathtub. His valet stood by holding heated towels.

For a while they talked of matters other than Louisiana. It was Napoleon who brought the subject up. He told them quietly of his intention to sell the colony to the United States. Then he went on scrubbing himself.

"I flatter myself," said Lucien, "that the Chambers will not give their consent."

Napoleon looked surprised. "You flatter yourself!" he said. "That is precious, in truth!"

Joseph muttered, "And I, too, flatter myself, as I have already told the First Consul."

"And what did I answer?" demanded Napoleon.

"That you would do it without the Chambers," admitted Joseph.

"Precisely!" cried Napoleon, his temper rising. "That is what I have taken the liberty of informing Monsieur Joseph, and what I now repeat to the Citizen Lucien, begging him at the same time to give me his opinion about it without taking into consideration his paternal tenderness for his diplomatic conquest."

Napoleon said much more, all of it filled with sarcasm and contempt. His two brothers were as ambitious as himself, but not as intelligent nor as aggressive. When he spoke of Lucien's "paternal tenderness for his diplomatic conquest" he meant the work Lucien had done in Spain to have Louisiana restored to France. Lucien had been bragging for a long time that it was he who had made Spain return the colony to France. He had been proud of this and now he did not want to see his work undone.

But it was Joseph who dared to threaten Napoleon. Bending over the bathtub, he said, "And you do well, my dear brother, not to expose your project to parliamentary discussion; for I declare to you that if necessary I will put myself at the head of the opposition which will not fail to be made against you."

Napoleon roared with laughter.

"Laugh, laugh, laugh then!" Joseph cried, his face bright red. "I will act up to my promise; and though I am not fond of mounting the tribunal, this time you will see me there!"

At this Napoleon sat up straight in the bathtub, and stared furiously at Joseph. How dare he threaten to oppose the plans of the First Consul, to talk of making speeches against him before the government!

"You will have no need to lead the opposition," Napoleon said coldly, "for I repeat there will be no debate, for the reason that the project which has not the fortune to meet your approval, conceived by me, negotiated by me alone, shall be ratified and executed by me alone, do you understand? By me, who laugh at your opposition!"

These were the words not of a First Consul of the Republic of France, but of a king and emperor. That was the way Napoleon was thinking of himself. It was to be ME! ME! He would consult with no body of government, but would do as he pleased.

"Good!" Joseph cried in answer. Then he referred to the people Napoleon had sent into exile. Joseph warned him that the same fate might happen to him, to all of them.

This was more than Napoleon could take from anyone, even his brother. He fell back in the tub. The sudden, angry movement sent the water splashing into the air and over the sides. Joseph was drenched, and Lucien had to wipe his face. "You are insolent!" Napoleon cried.

His valet, still standing by holding the hot towels, crashed to the floor in a faint.

Joseph went home to change his clothes, but Lucien stayed to talk further with Napoleon. In his later writings he told how he continued the same arguments Joseph had used, but in a calmer tone. He argued that Napoleon had no right to sell Louisiana without consulting the Chambers, that such a sale was breaking the French Constitution. Napoleon sneered at this argument.

"Go about your business!" he shouted at one point. "Constitution! Unconstitutional! Repub-

lic! National sovereignty! Big words! Great
phrases!"

Napoleon did try to convince Lucien that he
must sell Louisiana to the United States. He put
it on the grounds that he needed the money for
the war both knew would soon start with
England. He spoke of the failure of San Domingo. France could never hold her colonies in
the Western Hemisphere, he said. She could
never depend upon victories where a large navy
was needed.

It went on and on. At last Lucien accused
Napoleon of despising the French Constitution,
and added, ". . . seeing as you despise it thus, if
I were not your brother, I would be your enemy."

"My enemy!" yelled Napoleon, his temper
rising again. "Ah, I would advise you! My
enemy! That is a trifle strong!" He picked up a
snuff box and weighed it in his hand. "You my
enemy!" he cried again. "I would break you,
look, like this box!"

He threw the snuff box to the floor with all
his strength, smashing it to bits.

15: *Sold to America!*

AFTER LIVINGSTON'S MEETING WITH MAR-
bois, two weeks passed before anything else happened. During this time Monroe was sick. Livingston alone represented the United States, and
it would be a long time before he could hear
from Washington. A sailing ship must cross the

Atlantic and return with orders from the United States government before he could act. During this period he seems to have avoided contact with the French officials.

Napoleon himself broke the silence. He drew up a document that sold Louisiana to the United States. In return he was to be given fifteen million dollars together with the American government's agreement to favor French commerce.

On April 27 Marbois took this document to Monroe and Livingston. The three men conversed at great length. Monroe was still so weak from his illness that he had to lie on a couch all through the conference.

On April 30 Livingston and Monroe dined with Napoleon. He said little about the purchase, except that it must be settled quickly. On May 2 Monroe and Livingston signed the papers they had drawn up with Marbois. The sale still had to be approved by Jefferson and the United States Congress, of course, but otherwise Louisiana was sold!

Two weeks after this, on May 18, Napoleon declared war on Great Britain. The Peace of Amiens, begun in 1801, had lasted less than two years. Except for that brief breathing spell, the two nations were to fight each other, in all, for twenty-two years. It did not end until Napoleon's exile to St. Helena in 1815.

The fact that the entire Louisiana territory now belonged to the United States seemed almost beyond belief to many people. It was the greatest bargain in history. Suddenly, overnight the United States had doubled its size! Livingston made a speech in Paris, in which he said, in part:

"We have lived long, but this is the noblest work of our lives. . . . From this day the United States takes its place among the powers of the first rank. . . . The instruments we have just signed will cause no tears to be shed; they prepare ages of happiness for innumerable generations of human creatures. . . ."

Livingston was proud of his part in the Purchase and he had every right to be. Actually he could have completed the details without help from James Monroe because Napoleon had decided to sell Louisiana even before Monroe arrived in Paris. Later much of the credit was to go to Monroe, partly because James Madison did not like Livingston. Nevertheless, it was Livingston who was considered the leading American in the business connected with the Purchase.

During July the news and papers concerned with the sale reached Thomas Jefferson in Washington. As soon as the news got out, there was excitement all over the United States. Everyone talked of "America's extension of empire" and "the immortal Jefferson." Yet Jefferson, himself, was at first rather stunned by the news. He had wanted New Orleans and, if possible, the Floridas. Instead, the United States had received all this territory, no one knew quite how much.

For this was one of the most curious parts of the whole thing. No one seems to have been exactly certain about what the United States was buying! The details of the boundaries of Louisiana were not at all clear. Much of this unexplored territory was unknown.

At about the time Monroe had sailed for France, Jefferson had asked Meriwether Lewis to begin an exploration of the Missouri River, but even that had not got under way yet. Soon Lewis would begin his famous explorations of the whole Louisiana territory. Later he was to be joined by Captain William Clark.*

But for the moment no one knew what was

*You can read more about these explorations in another Landmark Book, *The Lewis and Clark Expedition* by Richard L. Neuberger.

included in Louisiana. Did it include Texas? At one point Jefferson was certain the colony stretched to the Rio Grande. At another it was thought to include even the Oregon! Most of these particular questions were, of course, to come later. Now the question was a general one. What really *was* Louisiana?

Even Spain had always been confused about this question. As we know, the Spanish officials were not too clear about just how much land they had given to France when that transaction took place. When Napoleon sold Louisiana to the United States he was just as uncertain as Spain had been.

Livingston, interested in learning whether the Floridas were included in the sale, had asked Talleyrand one question about the boundaries. It was, "What are the eastern bounds of Louisiana?"

These, in the extreme south, might take in the Floridas. Above New Orleans the eastern boundary was the Mississippi River and the United States itself.

"I do not know," was Talleyrand's answer to this question. "You must take it as we received it."

"But what did you mean to take?" asked Livingston.

"I do not know," said Talleyrand again.

"Then you mean that we shall construe it our own way?"

"I can give you no direction," said Talleyrand. "You have made a noble bargain for yourselves, and I suppose you will make the most of it."

This was, of course, the craftiness of Talleyrand. He knew full well that France did not own the Floridas, and so they could not be included in the sale. Although he did not want to admit it, the fact that the Floridas were not part of the Louisiana Purchase soon became clear to everyone.

Indeed, when news of the Purchase reached Washington it seemed for a while that Spain might prevent the whole transaction from taking place. Yrujo, the Spanish ambassador, informed Jefferson that France had no legal right to sell Louisiana. The last and final papers between Napoleon and Charles IV had never been signed. Down in New Orleans Laussat still waited for the formal transfer of the colony from Spain to France.

Since these matters had not taken place yet,

the Spanish ambassador claimed that Napoleon was selling what he did not own! Even if Napoleon did own it, Yrujo insisted, he had no right to sell it to any country. That had been one of the terms of his bargain with Spain.

Jefferson paid little attention to this dispute, and in the end it caused no real trouble. Charles IV of Spain, as usual, was not much interested in Louisiana. Anyway, there was nothing he could have done.

Naturally Jefferson was elated and overjoyed at the idea that the United States should include all Louisiana. But there were many problems still to be settled. He foresaw the fact that one day the nation would expand all the way to the Pacific Ocean, but he knew there was much to be overcome even before Louisiana was accepted as part of the country.

For Jefferson had now to take the matter of the Purchase to the Congress. No government business as important as this could be settled without consent from the representatives of the states. The President knew many of them would oppose him violently. Some of them really be-lieved the Purchase would be a mistake; some were his enemies and would take the other side of any matter which he favored.

Congress was not to meet until October, so all summer Jefferson tried to find out more about Louisiana. He sent lists of questions to anyone who might be able to furnish information, but there were few of these people and they did not know much. He read everything written about the colony, and tried in every other way to arm himself for the battle that was coming.

Even Jefferson was not sure Louisiana would become part of the United States in a true sense, at least not at once. He was not sure how all this land could be handled. He wrote, in a letter to a friend:

"I presume the island of N. Orleans and the settled country on the opposite bank, will be annexed to the Mississippi territory. ... The rest will probably be locked up from American settlement, and under the self-government of the native occupants."

We might suppose that at this time Jefferson thought that most of Louisiana would be left to the Indians, the native occupants. To dream that Americans would inhabit it all was beyond imagination, even to Jefferson.

16: *Jefferson and the Constitution*

AFTER THE FIRST SURPRISE CAUSED BY THE
willingness of Napoleon to part with Louisiana,
Jefferson began to worry about another very
important question. Did the Constitution of the
United States allow the government to buy this
territory? In private Jefferson admitted he was

not sure, and at least once he referred to the Purchase as "an act beyond the Constitution."

Was it really that? Historians and writers have argued about it for a hundred and fifty years, just as politicians and statesmen argued about it at the time.

It is true that the framers and authors of the Constitution did not foresee that the United States would ever include Louisiana. They seemed to have had no idea, and no wish, that the nation would ever be any larger than the thirteen original colonies. Indeed, our founding fathers considered the nation already so huge that it was expected each state would make its own laws and govern itself almost entirely. The central government in Washington, and before that in Philadelphia, was intended only to bind the states together. In thus being united they could protect themselves from interference by a foreign government.

Jefferson had a ticklish and delicate situation on his hands and he knew it. He loved and respected the Constitution as much as or more than any other man in the United States. Yet he could not let pass the country's opportunity to acquire Louisiana.

Furthermore, he had to act at once. There was a possibility that Napoleon might change his mind. There was danger that the Spanish might set up such a howl that the entire transaction would crumble to pieces. Jefferson summoned the Congress to meet in October to act upon the Purchase. The sooner he got it over with the better.

The article of the Constitution that worried Jefferson read, in part: "Congress shall have power to dispose of, and make all needful rules and regulations respecting the territory and other property belonging to the United States."

This meant lands owned at the time the Constitution was written. There was, it was true, nothing in it that said plainly that the United States could not buy new land. But there was nothing anywhere in the Constitution that stated that new territory *could* be bought. It seems reasonable now to believe that if the early framers of the Constitution had wanted to make it illegal for the United States to expand by buying territory outside the limits of the existing states they would have said so. They did not say so in any way at all.

Yet Jefferson did believe he was going beyond

his rights, and that the Constitution was being violated. It was a departure from his own most sacred principles. But he believed it was the will of the majority of the people that Louisiana be accepted, and that their representatives in Congress and in the Senate would favor the move. The only possible remedy, in Jefferson's view, was that there should be a new amendment to the Constitution permitting the United States to expand. He wrote one and presented it to his cabinet in August. They paid little attention to it, and it was never added to the original document.

All the opposition Jefferson had expected soon burst forth. It was strong and violent. The Federalists, led by Alexander Hamilton, accused Jefferson of tearing the Constitution to shreds. Many of the President's own party turned against him, too. There were those who said that France's rights and title to Louisiana were illegal or, at best, very doubtful. There were those who thought the price of fifteen million dollars was extremely high.

The real fear among those against the Purchase, however, sprang from something altogether different. This was that a number of agricultural states might be carved out of the territory, and that because of this, the rich eastern states would suffer huge losses. Some states even threatened to leave the Union.

This was the first time the United States had ever expanded, for the three states added to the original thirteen some years before had been carved out of the original thirteen. There was nothing to guide the lawmakers in their decisions. It is interesting to listen to some of the objections to buying Louisiana.

Even James Madison, the Secretary of State, was against Jefferson's proposal. He believed that ". . . no colony beyond the river (the Mississippi) could exist under the same government, but would infallibly give birth to a separate State, having in its bosom germs of collision with the East . . ."

A Senator Plumer, of New Hampshire, said, "Admit this western world into the Union and you destroy at once the weight and importance of the Eastern States and compel them to establish a separate, independent empire."

Alexander Hamilton, although he said Jefferson had wrecked the Constitution, and ridiculed the President for acting in a manner opposite to his own beliefs, was in favor of the Purchase. He suggested, also, that the United States seize the Floridas, if they could be had in no other way.

Fisher Ames seemed to think that by purchasing Louisiana the United States had bought a piece of the planet Mars or a slice of the moon. He wrote: "Now by adding an immeasurable world beyond the Mississippi, we rush like a comet into infinite space. In our wild career we may jostle some other world out of its orbit, but we shall in any event quench the light of our own."

Senator John Taylor, from Jefferson's own Virginia, said in the debate in the Senate that the Purchase of Louisiana was exactly like the deed of some tyrannical European country.

Perhaps the most curious suggestion made was that the Purchase be accepted, but that all Louisiana except New Orleans be sold to some "friendly European nation"!

There was much debating, too, about whether Louisiana should be taken simply as territory, or ruled over by the states as a possession, or whether it should, in time, be made a part of the United States. The Federalists were largely in favor of its being kept a possession. Thus Louisiana would become a kind of colonial empire, governed by the United States as it had been governed by Spain, but kept entirely separate from the states of the Union.

Despite all this, when the debates and arguments were ended and the Senate cast its vote on October 20, 1803, the vote was twenty-four to seven in favor of the Louisiana Purchase. Future details had still to be worked out, but this made Louisiana a part of the United States. Also it proved to all that the United States could expand and could purchase other territory.

Thus did the United States double its size. It was to be some time before it was decided just how much land was contained in the Louisiana Purchase, but when this was finally settled it was found that the nation had bought 883,072 square miles, or 565,166,080 acres, for fifteen million dollars. Louisiana had been purchased for about four cents an acre!

17: *The Reign of Twenty Days*

ALL THIS TIME PIERRE CLEMENT DE LAUSSAT, the French Prefect, was waiting in New Orleans. He was a man without power, for the Spanish still ruled the city. As yet there had been no formal transfer of Louisiana from Spain to France.

Rumors reached New Orleans as early as the late spring of 1803 that Napoleon was selling Louisiana, but belief in such tales was slow in developing. Such a thing seemed impossible. The Spanish argued that it could not be true, for Louisiana was not Napoleon's to sell. They had not even received instructions from Madrid to turn over rule of the colony to Laussat and the French.

The French Orleanians would not believe it either. To be sold to the United States! That was impossible! Yet Americans coming into the city talked of it more and more, and soon everyone in New Orleans was talking about it. At last some of the citizens and visiting dignitaries began to worry a great deal.

Of course Laussat still waited for the French army that was never to arrive. He remained in the same uncomfortable position all through the summer and fall.

At last word came from France that the transfer of the colony was to take place at once. With it, too, came the news that very soon the United States would take over Louisiana. It was embarrassing to Laussat, for he must now go through a change of government from Spain to France that would last only a very short time. Actually it lasted twenty days, and so has always been called the "reign of twenty days."

Talleyrand and Minister of the French Navy Decrès instructed Laussat to take charge of all ceremonies. However, they had been paying so little attention to him that they were not even sure he was still alive. In case Laussat "should be found dead," as Talleyrand put it, he sent a French officer, a Captain Landias, down from New York.

On November 23 Laussat met with the two Spanish officials, Governor Salcedo and the Marquis de Casa Calvo, to arrange for the ceremonies. The date was set for November 30 at noon. Laussat then selected a prominent citizen, Etienne de Boré, to serve as mayor, and chose a group of well-known Creoles to form a city council. It is said these gentlemen were not too pleased. It was sugar-grinding season, and some of them had almost to be dragged from their plantations!

At the proper hour on November 30 Laussat and the Spanish officials took their places on a platform in the council chamber of the Cabildo, or government house. There Governor Salcedo handed over to Laussat the keys to the forts of St. Charles and St. Louis, and turned over to him the chair of honor. Then they all stepped out on a balcony to watch the lowering of the Spanish flags in the Place d'Armes across the street, and the raising of French flags in their places.

Laussat then went down and over to the square where he accepted a pledge of loyalty from the town militia. Later he attended a meeting with Etienne de Boré, the city's first mayor, and the new town council

There was activity in other parts of the colony, too. The few French officers who had come over from France took charge of the Spanish posts along the Mississippi and throughout Lower Louisiana. The upper half of the territory, however, remained unoccupied by Napoleon's representatives.

But most of the excitement was in New Orleans. In his speech Laussat told the people that soon all who were willing would find themselves citizens of the United States. Those who wanted to leave, he said were free to do so. At the end of his talk he said, "May a Louisianian and a Frenchman never meet upon any spot of the earth without feeling tenderly drawn to each other, and without saluting each other with the title of brother!"

The Marquis Casa Calvo announced that Spanish subjects who did not wish to leave New Orleans and Louisiana might stay, that from then on they would owe no allegiance to Spanish rule.

The next day Laussat gave a big dinner for seventy-five French, Spanish and American guests. There were many speeches praising Napoleon Bonaparte, Charles IV of Spain, and Thomas Jefferson. After the dinner there was a great ball where the dancing lasted until ten o'clock in the morning.

For the next two weeks there was celebration after celebration. There were fireworks displays, balls, dances, and dinners. Now the Spanish, getting ready to depart, became extremely polite to Laussat, and he seemed to enjoy it all.

It must be said for Laussat that he carried out all his duties with dignity. He acted as if France were taking over Louisiana forever. As the celebration went on, Laussat, Mayor de Boré, and the city council worked hard. They met at least ten times during the first two weeks, writing new

city laws, some of which are still part of New
Orleans law today.

As Laussat had not had the best of treatment
during the months he had been in New Orleans,
it would be hard to blame him if he had cared
little about what happened to the city or its residents during the twenty days of his administra-
tion. Yet in those twenty days he gave New Orleans the first democratic government in its long
history.

The citizens of New Orleans enjoyed all the
festivities and they took part in the dancing and
celebrating. With all the music and fireworks
and fine speeches it must have been like the
Fourth of July and New Year's Eve combined.
Yet this excitement did not last or go very deep.

Most of the people had no real feeling about
this brief change from Spanish to French ownership. Very few planned to leave the city. French
and Spanish, and many of them by now a mix-
ture of the two nationalities, they had their
homes, their businesses, and their lives in New
Orleans. Most of them had been born there. To
leave would have meant tearing up their lives
by the roots. They neither rejoiced nor grieved
at this changing of laws and governments.

The only ones who did grieve were those who had long been admirers of Napoleon Bonaparte. They were disappointed that the city was not to remain a French colony. There were a great many of these people, although they were but a small part of the whole population of New Orleans.

But these Bonapartists, as they were called, made up with enthusiasm whatever they lacked in numbers. Amongst them were many of the leading citizens of the city. To these people Napoleon was the greatest genius of all time. What they had been longing for had come to pass: they were now citizens of Napoleon's France. But their French citizenship was to last only twenty days! No wonder the Bonapartists were shocked and bitter.

18: *The Transfer to the United States*

WHILE ALL THIS WAS GOING ON DOWN IN New Orleans the men in Washington still worried about what was to be done with Louisiana. They still talked about an amendment to the Constitution to make the Purchase legal. Senator John Quincy Adams of Massachusetts, the son of the second President of the United States, who would become the sixth President himself one day, drafted one amendment and presented it to Secretary of State James Madison. Madison did not accept it. He suggested that there be only a simple statement, to read, "Louisiana is hereby admitted into this Union."

So Louisiana was accepted without a Constitutional amendment, but as if it had been received through treaty with a foreign power. It was declared a territory, a possession, that was not to become a part of the United States.

A line was drawn dividing it into two parts, the same line which today divides the State of Arkansas from the State of Louisiana. The territory above the line, and stretching all the way north to the Canadian border, was named the District of Louisiana. The southern part, which had almost the same boundaries as the present State of Louisiana, and which of course included New Orleans, was to be known as the Territory of Orleans. How much land this included, no one knew exactly. Was West Florida part of it? Texas? That was left for the future to decide.

Provision was made for the Territory of Orleans to become part of the United States proper at some future date. Nothing was said about the northern part of the colony, or what was now called the District of Louisiana. The reason for this was that the northern part had so few white settlers. It was still Indian country.

But the Territory of Orleans contained more than fifty thousand people of European background. It had an old and civilized society.

So the treaty stated that "the inhabitants of the ceded territory shall be incorporated in the Union of the United States, and admitted as soon as possible, according to the principles of the Federal Constitution, to the enjoyment of all the rights, advantages, and immunities of citizens of the United States; and in the meantime they shall be maintained and protected in the free enjoyment of their liberty, property, and the religion they profess."

The man who had been governor of the Mississippi Territory, W. C. C. Claiborne, was sent to New Orleans as governor of the Territory of Orleans. General James Wilkinson was appointed governor of the District of Louisiana.

Claiborne and Wilkinson were in New Orleans some time before the formal transfer of Louisiana from France to the United States.

They met with Laussat and arrangements were made.

Laussat's twenty days of rule came to an end on December 20, 1803, when the official transfer took place. The ceremonies were held in the same place where Spain, less than three weeks before, had handed the colony over to France, in front of the old Cabildo and in the Place d'Armes. (Now the Place d'Armes is called Jackson Square.)

What sights that square in New Orleans had seen during its long history! Here Bienville, founder of New Orleans, had established his parade grounds in which to march his ragged troops. Here slaves and captured Indians had walked in chains. Here had been held both executions and celebrations. Here "Bloody" O'Reilly had seized the city for Spain. Here Laussat had received it back from Spain in the name of France. Now, on exactly the same spot, Louisiana and New Orleans were to become American property.

At eleven o'clock on the morning of December 20, United States troops, who had come down the river to take part in the event, formed in ranks in the square. All about the area, in the streets, on all the balconies, even on rooftops, the citizens of New Orleans watched.

Having signed their names to the necessary documents, Laussat and the Spanish officials, wearing elaborate costumes and plumed hats, came out of the Cabildo. With them were Claiborne and General Wilkinson, dressed in their plainer American garb. Claiborne, Wilkinson and Laussat stepped to the front and waited a moment. Suddenly there was a loud shout of "Hurrah!" from the Americans in the crowd. Hats waved, a few Americans applauded.

But that was all. There was not a sound from the Creole residents of New Orleans. It was as if they had planned it. They stood in utter silence. Claiborne told later of the odd feeling he had at that moment. He felt their resentment and bitterness that they were being torn away from France.

Laussat turned deathly pale.

In the square, it was Laussat who spoke first. He addressed the town militia.

"Militiamen of New Orleans and of Louisiana," he said in clear and ringing tones, "in these last days you have given proof of your great zeal and your filial devotion to the French flag during the brief time that it has waved above your shores. This I shall convey to France and to her government, and in their name I thank you."

Then Laussat took a place beside the pole on which fluttered the flag of the French Republic and said, "To the commissaries of the United States, here present, I now transmit your commandment; obey them henceforth as the representatives of your legitimate government."

These words presented the Colony of Louisiana to the government of the United States.

Now Claiborne stepped forward, his face serious, for there was still that complete silence all about him. He spoke calmly and quietly, and at the end he said:

"The cession confers upon you and your descendants the full heritage of liberty; the benefit of fixed laws and of magistrates whom you yourselves will elect."

But even this promise of freedom, liberty, and democracy brought no answer from the crowds of Orleanians. They had never ruled themselves and they did not want to do so now.

The French flag was lowered slowly, and the American flag rose as slowly in its place. It was only then the quiet broke, and that was worse. In the crowd both men and women broke into sobs.

A French naval officer received the flag of France. He wrapped it around himself and carried it in silence to a French army officer, Sergeant-major Legrand. Legrand took the flag gently and wrapped it about his own body and carried it from the square. As he passed the American troops they presented arms and saluted to the solemn rolling of drums. Legrand was escorted by sixty young men as he departed the scene.

When Laussat spoke again his voice was trembling with emotion. "French citizens," he cried, "I shall inform the French government of the patriotic feeling with which you have today, two thousand five hundred leagues from her shores, fulfilled a religious duty towards this flag. I ask your commander to give me your names that I may place them before the First Consul."

With that Laussat himself burst into tears, turned and left in haste.

That evening Laussat gave a dinner at which there were four hundred and fifty guests. There were more speeches, followed by toasts to the

United States and Thomas Jefferson, to Napoleon and the Republic of France, to Charles IV and Spain, and to the future happiness of Louisiana. Afterwards there was a ball at which the guests again danced all night long.

These festivities continued until January 3, 1804, when a ball was given in honor of Madame Laussat, wife of the French Commissioner.

But the people of New Orleans were far from happy. They had greeted the transfer of Louisiana to the United States with tears. Later, the tears dry, they watched the changes that took place with mounting anger.

This is not so hard to understand. In less than a month their form of government had been changed from Spanish to French to American. To them American laws and ways were the strangest of all and they did not like them.

They knew nothing of democracy. Spanish rule had not been harsh for some years, but nevertheless the Spanish governors had ruled almost like kings, carrying out the orders of His Majesty's government in Madrid. The Bonapartists in New Orleans had wanted to be citizens of the France of Napoleon. Yet in their hearts they had known that France would not be a republic much longer.

They had realized that the First Consul would soon wipe out all pretenses of a republican form of government and declare himself emperor.

Also, these New Orleans Creoles—people of French or Spanish background—had never liked Americans as a whole. They were a gentle, sensitive, cultured people. They thought the Americans rough and coarse in their manners and speech. But the worst part of all perhaps was the usage of the English language in New Orleans, which began almost as soon as the transfer took place. From then on all official business and the courts of law were conducted in English. Many Creole families swore they would never speak English nor allow their children to learn it.

Moreover, though they had been promised full equality and liberty with other Americans, their section was not yet a state of the Union. It was a territory of the United States, which was entirely different. The Orleanians felt they had been sold, without their consent, to a foreign nation. For a while it seemed that they had no country at all.

Claiborne, the American governor of the territory of Orleans, soon found himself the victim of all kinds of attacks. The newspapers that were still printed in French contained articles and editorials denouncing him and his officials as villains. He was insulted on the streets by the coolness of the citizens. Many New Orleans families of prominence closed the doors of their homes to all Americans and would not invite them to their social affairs.

There were even duels between Creoles and Americans. Quarrels and fights occurred at balls and in places of public entertainment. Creoles would not let their children play with American children. They forbade their daughters and sons to marry Americans. This was to go on for many years.

At first Claiborne did not seem to understand the people of New Orleans. He did not trust them. It was fortunate, he thought, that Napoleon was busy with wars in Europe, for Claiborne firmly believed that the Orleanians would side with France in case of war between France and the United States. In this he was very probably quite right.

But Claiborne, a Virginia gentleman with pleasant manners, did win some friends in New Orleans. Eventually, his wife having died, he married again into an old French family of the city.

Years later, in 1812, when the State of Louisiana was formed and admitted to the Union, Claiborne was elected governor of the state. This was proof of the great popularity he had won, for he had run against James Villeré, son of the Villeré who had been killed by the order of "Bloody" O'Reilly. At the time of this election Claiborne had been governor of the Territory of Orleans for more than eight years. He went straight from that position to the one to which he had been elected by people who had formerly hated him. But that was all far in the future when the transfer of Louisiana took place.

Laussat remained in New Orleans for four months after he had played his part in the transfer. He aided Claiborne and even took his side now and then when the governor was attacked. When he found that many lies were being told about the Americans, he tried his best to straighten out some of these differences. He also made an effort to improve the understanding between the old residents of the city and the newly arrived officials.

There were even citizens who asked Laussat

if he did not think Napoleon might take Louisiana back after he had finished the war with England. A very honest man, Laussat told these people frankly that it would be unwise to imagine such a thing. Never again would New Orleans belong to a European power, he would tell them. Their bitterness would die. Soon they would realize the advantages of being part of the United States.

It may even be that Laussat left New Orleans with sincere regret. When he sailed on April 21, 1804, his last words were: "It is a hard thing for me, having once known this land, to part from it."

On the other hand, it may only have been French politeness.

19: *Thomas Jefferson Looks Ahead*

IN THE BEGINNING OF THE YEAR 1804 THERE were still many sides to the Louisiana question for Jefferson to consider. He had to turn them over and over in his mind to decide upon each issue concerning this new territory. His enemies found that the Purchase gave them excuse after excuse to criticize him.

This man, who above all loved freedom and democracy, was now called a tyrant. It continued to be said that he had violated the Constitution. It was said that with the Purchase the United States had ceased to be a republic of free and independent states and that Jefferson had now put the nation on its way to becoming an empire. He was called a hypocrite by the Federalists, who claimed he had not lived up to his own beliefs as stated in both the Declaration of Independence and the Constitution. He was compared to Napoleon.

Many members of the Congress and the Senate disapproved of the way Louisiana was being handled. The power given the governors was thought by some to be as great as that of kings. Other speakers said that the people of Louisiana had been deprived of all liberty.

On another side were those who thought the citizens of Louisiana should have no rights at all. These Congressmen and Senators thought that Louisianians ought to be treated like the citizens of a conquered nation. Too, there were still those from the states along the Atlantic seaboard who complained that if Louisiana were ever settled and cultivated the farmers and planters of their states would be ruined. Some others feared New Orleans and thought it should be kept under close watch, for it was considered to be a stronghold of piracy, smuggling, and other evils.

So again Jefferson had to call upon his patience. He must have remembered that if he had listened to some of these very same gentlemen a few years before, many unfortunate things might have come to pass. The United States might have been pulled into a war with France; the Mississippi River might have remained closed to American shipping; and New Orleans might never have become an American port.

As usual he moved slowly, taking his time, planning carefully. He foresaw that New Orleans and the area surrounding it would form a state of the Union in the near future, but he did not believe the people of that city were ready for statehood yet.

Early in 1804 a delegation arrived in Washington with the demand that the New Orleans vicinity be made a state. For the moment they were refused.

As for the rest of Louisiana, the Lewis and Clark explorations had begun. Before any move could be made or any decision reached concerning that wilderness, more must be known about it. There were parts of it into which no white man had ever ventured.

And of course Jefferson's enemies and those who disagreed with him tried their best to defeat him when he ran for re-election late in 1804. However, as proof that most of the citizens of the country were with Jefferson and in favor of the Louisiana Purchase, he was elected to a second term, and again in March 1805 took an oath of office as President for his second term.

Throughout 1804 and 1805 most of the argument about Louisiana continued to be about its boundaries. The Spaniards stopped protesting that the United States had no rights in Louisiana at all. Instead, they made efforts to limit the area that had been bought. Jefferson had hoped, and perhaps thought, that Louisiana stretched to the Rio Grande River separating Texas and Mexico. He had been inclined to believe it included at least West Florida, if not both Floridas. Spain denied these claims vigorously.

Spanish authorities on the North American continent became increasingly angry as time went on. All through 1804 Spanish officials and troops remained in New Orleans. Claiborne asked them to depart a number of times, but they refused. The American governor became more and more suspicious of them. He was convinced the Marquis de Casa Calvo was sending messages to the Spanish governor of Texas and to Spanish authorities in the Floridas concerning American plans and American exploration expeditions.

At last, at Claiborne's insistence, the Spanish troops were sent to Pensacola, but Casa Calvo and the other officials remained. In the summer of 1805 a rumor spread through New Orleans that Louisiana had been given back to Spain by the United States. It was suspected that Casa Calvo had started this rumor in order to cause trouble.

All this time the Spanish in America believed that war between Spain and the United States would start at any moment. They believed the United States planned to seize the Floridas by force. A squadron of Spanish warships was actually waiting at Havana, Cuba with orders to blockade American ports, the mouth of the Mississippi, and those of the Potomac and Delaware. Forts were established along the Texas border.

The United States also took military measures. Troops were sent to the forts along the Mississippi. Reinforcements were sent to St. Louis and to New Orleans. In February 1806 Jefferson ordered Casa Calvo dismissed from Louisiana. The Spanish officials departed with reluctance, but remained in the Floridas for some time. Later Casa Calvo watched from Texas.

As we know, no war broke out then. There were disagreeable incidents along the Texas border and in other places, but never an official war with Spain. The boundary dispute was to go on for years. So it was 1819 before the Floridas became part of American territory, and 1845 before Texas joined the Union.

During his second term of office Jefferson had even more serious problems to face than in his first one. It was a time of great crisis for the United States, one filled with political troubles. The country was under great strain caused by states attempting to separate from the Union, and by the ambitions of dangerous men who wanted personal power and wealth.

But through it all Jefferson worked to keep the United States together. He also continued the explorations of Louisiana, of its area and limits and wealth, its mountains and rivers and great forests. He saw that it was America's destiny to grow and expand. Above all, she must free herself from the danger of allowing unfriendly European powers to hold territory close to her borders.

Jefferson continued to do everything possible to buy the Floridas, which at the moment seemed the most valuable Spanish possession next door to the United States. He sent James Monroe to Spain in 1804. Discussions with the Spanish government went on through 1805. But nothing was gained.

At least a part of the reason for Spain's refusal to sell the Floridas was due to the attitude of Napoleon. More than ever now Napoleon hoped the United States and Spain would go to war. It must have seemed to him that his plan to bring this war about was working out perfectly. Back in Paris Monroe had no trouble in discovering this.

Napoleon was now Emperor of France, for he had crowned himself and taken that title on May 18, 1804. Concerning him, Talleyrand wrote American officials:

"His Imperial Majesty has seen with pain the

United States commence their differences with Spain in an unusual manner, and conduct themselves toward the Floridas by acts of violence which, not being founded on right, could have no other effect but to injure its lawful owners."

Of course this was hypocrisy.

Napoleon had no intention of allowing Spain to sell the Floridas to the United States. Some historians believe if war had come then between the United States and Spain, Napoleon would have tried to seize Louisiana for himself. In the end, in 1808, the King of Spain was tricked into abdicating, and Joseph Bonaparte was made the new king by his brother. When this happened the Spanish people revolted, the English invaded Spain, and it all led to Napoleon's end as a conqueror.

While all this went on there was more and more trouble in New Orleans. Some residents left the city and went to live in Spanish territory rather than live under the American government. The ardent Bonapartists, delighted that Napoleon was Emperor of France, boasted with even more enthusiasm about their hero.

When an American newspaper began publishing in the city and printed articles attacking

Napoleon, these citizens, led by the new French Consul, were so furious that a riot almost took place. Claiborne wrote James Madison that these people threatened to rise and massacre the printer.

Yet when the Fourth of July was celebrated in the city for the first time, Americans there carried on with so much patriotism that Claiborne was overjoyed. He wrote Madison again, and told of his renewed hopes that New Orleans would become an American city one day.

During this same period Jefferson kept receiving reports of many Americans who wanted to cross the Mississippi River and establish homes in Louisiana.

20: *Here Come the Americans!*

CONGRESS HAD PROMISED STATEHOOD TO the Territory of Orleans when its population reached sixty thousand. From the day of the Purchase its growth was rapid. As soon as New Orleans and the surrounding area became part of the United States, Americans poured in.

The population of the city had been about

ten thousand in 1803. By 1811 this had increased to more than thirty-three thousand, and the Territory of Orleans contained about fifty thousand persons. Now a committee was formed under the leadership of a rich planter named Julien Poydras, and Congress was asked once more that the territory be made a state of the United States.

Again there was strong opposition in Washington. Some members of Congress said that it would be like taking a foreign country into the Union. They protested that too many citizens of the Territory of Orleans were still French and Spanish at heart, that they did not even speak the English language. Josiah Quincy of Massachusetts went so far as to declare that if this territory was admitted to the United States as a state the other states should withdraw from the Union, ". . . violently if they must."

Despite this, the bill asking that the Territory of Orleans be made a state passed Congress. In January 1812 a convention to form a state constitution was held in New Orleans. Congress approved the constitution that was written, and the new state was admitted to the Union on April 8, 1812.

As the first section of the Colony of Louisiana

to become a state with full rights, it was given the name of the State of Louisiana. Its boundaries were almost exactly as they are today. After that the rest of the colony, until then known as the District of Louisiana, was usually called the Missouri Territory to avoid confusion with the State of Louisiana.

Americans now far outnumbered the French and Spanish Creoles in New Orleans and the surrounding country, yet much feeling against the United States and Americans remained. This did not begin to disappear until all the citizens of New Orleans united on the plantation battlefields of Chalmette. There, at the close of the War of 1812, they successfully defended the city from invasion by the British. This battle brought all the nationalities in the city together as one people and wiped out the more important of their many differences.

The followers of Napoleon in New Orleans remained his admirers until the end. There is an interesting tale told in New Orleans about them.

After the Battle of Waterloo, when the French were defeated by the English and the fortunes of Napoleon collapsed, the Emperor was exiled to the Island of St. Helena. When news of this reached New Orleans in 1815 a group of Creoles became excited and began to plan to rescue Napoleon from his island prison.

The mayor of New Orleans, Nicholas Girod, was one of the leaders of the group. Mayor Girod offered his own home to be used as a residence by Napoleon if he could be brought to the city. Then a rescue party was organized under the leadership of the ex-pirate and hero of the Battle of New Orleans, Dominique You. This colorful individual had also been chief lieutenant of Jean Lafitte* and had served under General Andrew Jackson at Chalmette.

We will never know now if the scheme would have succeeded, for Napoleon died before the expedition sailed from New Orleans. Mayor Girod's house still stands in New Orleans, and is now known as the "Napoleon House."

After the State of Louisiana was formed, even those members of Congress who disliked the idea must have realized that other states would soon be carved out of the colony bought from Napoleon. These states, too, would become part of the United States.

The size of this territory, when explored and

*You can read more about this great adventurer in another Landmark Book, *The Pirate Lafitte and the Battle of New Orleans* by Robert Tallant.

measured, and its boundaries settled, continued to amaze all Americans. It was difficult to believe that nearly a million square miles had been added to the area of the nation. This territory was seven times larger than England, Scotland and Ireland combined. It was larger than France, Germany, Italy, Spain and Portugal combined.

It was indeed its size that frightened most of those who objected to the Louisiana Purchase. They had predicted this meant the end of the United States. Of course it meant exactly the opposite. It had changed many American ideas and policies, and shocked some of the signers of the Constitution. Yet, the Purchase was really the beginning of the United States as a leader among the nations of the earth.

Eventually—besides the State of Louisiana—the states of Arkansas, Iowa, Missouri, Nebraska, North and South Dakota, Oklahoma, and much of Kansas, Minnesota, Colorado, Montana and Wyoming were created from what had been the Colony of Louisiana.

Following a principle that had been set down as early as 1787 in the Northwest Ordinance, a territory was considered eligible far statehood when it could boast a population of sixty thousand or more.

After Louisiana the next state formed was Missouri, which was declared one of the United States in 1821. Then came Arkansas in 1836. Iowa was made a state in 1846, Minnesota in 1858, Kansas in 1861, Nebraska in 1867, Colorado in 1876, Montana and North and South Dakota in 1889, and Wyoming in 1890. The last was Oklahoma, long Indian Territory, which joined the others as a state in 1907. There were thirteen in all. The same number that had made up the original states of the nation!

The Americans came fast, crossing the Mississippi in great streams as more and more territory was opened for settlement. This was the gateway to the west, opened at last! The newcomers drove the Indians farther toward the Pacific each year. Towns were founded and in time some of them became great cities. At last, of course, the Rockies were crossed, and the United States reached to the shores of the Pacific Ocean itself.

As the years passed, objections to American expansion faded. Florida became a part of the

United States, then Texas, and at last the great lands of the West, and California and the Oregon Territory. Then the United States took on the boundaries it has today.

Some of the American leaders who were important in working out the details of the Louisiana Purchase continued to serve the United States in many ways.

At the end of his second term Thomas Jefferson retired to Monticello. He lived to be a strong and hearty eighty-three, riding horseback every day even in his old age. He never lost his interest in public affairs or in what was going on in the country, and he advised many of those who followed him in attempting to solve national problems.

As we know, James Madison, James Monroe, and John Quincy Adams all became Presidents of their country. Madison served in that office all through the difficult War of 1812. While he was President, Monroe increased the area of the United States by acquiring the Floridas. Monroe also wrote the Monroe Doctrine, one of the most important documents we possess, which forever

prevented any foreign power from owning territory in the Western Hemisphere.

As to those who opposed the Louisiana Purchase, most of them faded into obscurity.

On the other side of the Atlantic Ocean,
change came quickly. We know that by the time
of Napoleon's death on St. Helena, not only his
dream of empire ended, but also almost all
French ownership of land in the Americas.

The end of Spain's empire on this side of the
world began with the Louisiana Purchase, too.
It is true the Monroe Doctrine was to hasten
this, but it was the Purchase that started the
destruction of Spanish might in this hemisphere.
Through the years that followed, Mexico and
country after country in Central and South
America followed the lead of those parts of the
United States that had once been Spanish in
establishing free and independent governments.

So it may be said that it was the Louisiana
Purchase that gave most of the countries of this
hemisphere their start in winning the freedoms
they have today. It may be said that the Purchase
began the process that at last liberated the
Americas from European tyranny. Because of
the Purchase one country after another in the

Western Hemisphere ceased being a colony and became a nation.

As for the United States itself, the Purchase was the actual beginning of both real security and growth. It is true the first thirteen states had already won their independence. Yet if this country had remained small, with foreign colonies lying at its very borders, that independence would always have been in peril. It was Thomas Jefferson's Louisiana Purchase that made this country the great one it is in our time.

Index